New Directions for Institutional Research

J. Fredericks Volkwein
EDITOR-IN-CHIEF

Robert K. Toutkoushian
ASSOCIATE EDITOR

Assessing Character Outcomes in College

Jon C. Dalton
Terrence R. Russell
Sally Kline
EDITORS

Number 122 • Summer 2004
Jossey-Bass
San Francisco

ASSESSING CHARACTER OUTCOMES IN COLLEGE
Jon C. Dalton, Terrence R. Russell, Sally Kline (eds.)
New Directions for Institutional Research, no. 122
J. Fredericks Volkwein, Editor-in-Chief

NEW DIRECTIONS FOR INSTITUTIONAL RESEARCH (ISSN 0271-0579, electronic ISSN 1536-075X) is part of The Jossey-Bass Higher and Adult Education Series and is published quarterly by Wiley Subscription Services, Inc., A Wiley Company, at Jossey-Bass, 989 Market Street, San Francisco, California 94103-1741 (publication number USPS 098-830). Periodicals Postage Paid at San Francisco, California, and at additional mailing offices. POSTMASTER: Send address changes to New Directions for Institutional Research, Jossey-Bass, 989 Market Street, San Francisco, California 94103-1741.

SUBSCRIPTIONS cost $80.00 for individuals and $150.00 for institutions, agencies, and libraries. See order form at end of book.

EDITORIAL CORRESPONDENCE should be sent to J. Fredericks Volkwein, Center for the Study of Higher Education, Penn State University, 400 Rackley Building, University Park, PA 16801-5252.

New Directions for Institutional Research is indexed in *College Student Personnel Abstracts, Contents Pages in Education,* and *Current Index to Journals in Education* (ERIC).

Microfilm copies of issues and chapters are available in 16mm and 35mm, as well as microfiche in 105mm, through University Microfilms Inc., 300 North Zeeb Road, Ann Arbor, Michigan 48106-1346.

www.josseybass.com

CONTENTS

EDITORS' NOTES

Aristotle believed that character can best be developed through habit and regular practice of virtuous behavior. Since Aristotle, there has been much debate about the meaning of character and the most effective ways in which to encourage its development in the educational setting. American higher education has a long-standing concern for character development that is deeply rooted in the liberal arts tradition. The earliest American colleges were established to promote religious and moral education, and concern about character as an important outcome of higher education has continued to the present time.

Recent concern about the moral and civic values of college graduates and their ethical readiness to assume leadership and civic roles in society has focused renewed attention on the issue of character development in higher education. What does the construct of character mean in the context of the learning and student development objectives of contemporary colleges and universities? What educational priority should development of character have in the current purposes of higher education? Perhaps the most difficult question of all, What are the most effective measures for assessing character outcomes of college? For these and other reasons, it is increasingly important today for colleges and universities to document the contributions they make to character development during the college years.

Assessing character outcomes is one of the many research tasks that institutional researchers are called upon to do. As Richard A. Yanikoski describes in Chapter Two of this volume, character outcomes have significant implications for many college and university priorities, such as recruitment, accreditation, campus life, institutional credibility, and social improvement. Institutional researchers are routinely called upon to provide information for institutional leaders, analyze data on student experiences, and develop performance measures. Institutional research practitioners typically conduct such research either by developing their own in-house surveys or by using national survey data, notably the Cooperative Institutional Research Project (CIRP) and the National Student Survey of Engagement (NSSE). Institutional researchers use national student surveys in part to collect data on student experiences that may not be available from student records. Chapters Three, Four, and Five of this volume illustrate how such data can be useful for these research purposes.

In this volume, the authors examine character and its development from several perspectives and illustrate approaches to defining and assessing character outcomes in the higher education setting. The timeless debate about how to best encourage moral and civic learning in the educational process will not be resolved by what appears in these chapters, but it will hopefully expand the current dialogue about the meaning, relevance, and assessment of character in the educational efforts of American colleges and universities.

Jon C. Dalton
Terrence R. Russell
Sally Kline
Editors

JON C. DALTON is associate professor of higher education and director of the Hardee Center for Leadership and Ethics at the Florida State University.

TERRENCE R. RUSSELL is executive director of the Association for Institutional Research at the Florida State University.

SALLY KLINE is associate director of the Hardee Center for Leadership and Ethics at the Florida State University.

1

The authors examine the importance of character development in higher education today and the challenges of assessing this complex educational outcome.

Introduction

Jon C. Dalton, Anita Fitzgerald Henck

In his landmark work, *College,* Ernest Boyer wrote that "we need educated men and women who not only pursue their own personal interests but are also prepared to fulfill their social and civic obligations. And it is during the undergraduate experience, perhaps more than at any other time, that these essential qualities of mind and character are refined" (1987, p. 7).

Boyer argued that higher education must be a place not only to cultivate the habits of the mind but also to educate for character, transmit values, and provide a forum of preparation for citizenship, leadership, and responsible behavior. Others (Wingspread Group on Higher Education, 1993; Kellogg Commission on the Future of State and Land-Grant Universities, 2000) have contended that colleges and universities fail in their responsibility to prepare graduates for citizenship and moral leadership by ignoring questions of character and values in undergraduate education. In retrospect, nearly two decades later higher education has in fact made progress in responding to the Boyer call by focusing on reform of the curriculum and co-curriculum to enhance both intellectual and ethical development. Efforts to connect what Boyer referred to as "mind and character"—the holistic development of intellectual and ethical competencies—are at the forefront of progressive collegiate education for the twenty-first century.

Two important current challenges for promoting character in higher education are (1) achieving a better understanding of the complex interrelationships of intellectual, affective, and behavioral factors that contribute to development of moral character and (2) determining the most appropriate measures for assessing character outcomes. Character, like other complex holistic outcomes of higher education, is not easily defined or assessed. Some of the most important outcomes of college (character, identity,

New Directions for Institutional Research, no. 122, Summer 2004   © Wiley Periodicals, Inc.

integrity, emotional maturity, empathy, citizenship, the capacity to love and be loved, spiritual growth) do not easily lend themselves to empirical observation and description. Yet these outcomes are critical for a satisfying life and productive citizenship and are among the most important outcomes for higher education in the twenty-first century. They represent some of the fundamental ways in which higher education contributes to and improves the greater society it serves.

American higher education has always been deeply invested in the development of character as an outcome of the college experience. The notion of character is imbedded in the most basic concepts of liberal education, public service, and student development. Boyer's linking of mind and character reflected a traditional goal of American higher education: to promote learning in the context of personal integrity and social responsibility. Educating for character generally involved teaching students how to make intellectual judgments within a framework of values oriented to the public good and developing personal qualities of virtue and the strength of will to act in accordance with those values. The concept of character therefore encompasses both the intellectual and behavioral domains and connects student learning and personal development. Promoting character today, as in the past, entails not only strengthening students' capacities for rigorous thinking and ethical decision making but also helping them commit to a personal lifestyle that consistently incorporates moral reflection and judgment. James Hunter described character as "the autonomy to make ethical decisions always on behalf of the common good and the discipline to abide by that principle" (2000, p. 17).

Although character, empathy, citizenship, and the like reflect some of the most important outcomes of higher education, they are often not included in institutional assessment efforts because of their construct complexity and difficulty in measurement. Consequently, too much attention may be given to assessing those outcomes that are convenient while neglecting outcomes such as character that may be more relevant to the core mission of the institution. Alexander Astin notes this propensity in his comment that assessment "should not be concerned about values that can be measured but, instead, about measuring that which is valued" (in Banta, Lund, Black, and Oblander, 1996, p. 5).

This volume investigates approaches to defining character in the higher education setting and reports on several national and institutional efforts to assess aspects of character development. Several of the chapters were based on papers presented at the 2003 Institute on College Student Values, held February 3–5 at Florida State University. The theme of the institute focused on strategies for assessing character outcomes in higher education. In soliciting writings for this volume, the editors sought to address four broad issues related to the topic:

1. Reflections on leadership issues and challenges related to promoting character development as an educational priority in the higher education setting
2. Review of the historical context and meaning of character development in higher education in the United States
3. Examination of outcomes of character development using data from large national studies of college student learning and development
4. Review of institution-based outcomes assessment studies of character-related values, beliefs, and behaviors

The chapters have been organized to address these four broad issues pertaining to character education. In Chapter Two, Richard Yanikoski examines why educational leaders are voicing increasing support for attending to the moral, ethical, and civic development of college students and what can be done to enhance these efforts. In Chapter Three, C. Carney Strange addresses the role of character development in the college experience, the dimensions that constitute it, and various methods to assess its outcomes.

Chapters Four, Five, and Six examine aspects of character development in college using data from national studies of college student characteristics. In Chapter Four, George D. Kuh and Paul D. Umbach examine the college conditions that contribute to character development, using data from the National Survey of Student Engagement (NSSE). In Chapter Five, Helen S. Astin and Anthony Lising Antonio assess the kind of college experience that affects students' development of character. In Chapter Six, Linda J. Sax explores civic commitment among college students and offers strategies for how colleges can best prepare students for a life as a caring and involved citizen.

Chapters Seven and Eight look at institutional efforts to assess character development in the context of their institutional mission and goals. In Chapter Seven, Joseph W. Filkins and Joseph R. Ferrari report on findings from a universitywide values research project that connects students' attitudes and behaviors about institutional mission and values to their perceived impact. In Chapter Eight, Gay L. Holcomb and Arthur J. Nonneman examine the environments and experiences that are most conducive to growth in faith in their Faithful Change Research Project.

In the *Meno*, Plato wrote, "Can you tell me, Socrates, does virtue come from teaching? Or does it come not from teaching but from practice? Or does it come to people neither from practice nor from being learnt, but by nature or in some other way?" (*The Dialogues of Plato*, 1995, p. 35).

The ancient debate about how mind and character are connected and the role education should play in the development of ethical thinking and behavior continues today with greater urgency than it has had for some time. We hope that this volume will add to our understanding about how colleges and universities can play a greater role in achieving Boyer's vision of educating men and women who not only pursue their own personal interests but are also prepared to fulfill their social and civic obligations.

References

Banta, T. W., Lund, J. P., Black, K. E., and Oblander, F. W. *Assessment in Practice: Putting Principles to Work on College Campuses*. San Francisco: Jossey-Bass, 1996.

Boyer, E. L. *College: The Undergraduate Experience in America*. New York: HarperCollins, 1987.

Hunter, J. D. *The Death of Character: On the Moral Education of America's Children*. New York: Basic Books, 2000.

Kellogg Commission on the Future of State and Land-Grant Universities. *Renewing the Covenant: Learning, Discovery and Engagement in a New Age and Different World*. Washington, D.C.: National Association of State Universities and Land Grant Colleges, 2000.

Plato. *Meno. The Dialogues of Plato*. New York: Collier, 1995.

Wingspread Group on Higher Education. *An American Imperative: Higher Expectations for Higher Education* (1st ed.). Racine, Wis.: Johnson Foundation, 1993.

JON C. DALTON *is associate professor in educational leadership at Florida State University in Tallahassee. He also serves as the director of the Hardee Center for Leadership and Ethics at FSU.*

ANITA FITZGERALD HENCK *is vice president for student development and retention at Eastern Nazarene College in Quincy, Massachusetts. In addition, she holds the rank of professor, teaching in the undergraduate psychology program, as well as in the graduate higher education administration program at ENC.*

2

The author examines why educational leaders are voicing increasing support for attending to the moral, ethical, and civic development of college students and what can be done to enhance these efforts.

Leadership Perspectives on the Role of Character Development in Higher Education

Richard Yanikoski

For as long as intelligent people have considered the purposes of higher learning, character development has been a desirable if uneasy companion of intellectual growth. Aristotle observed long before the origin of the modern university that mankind in general and educators in particular have struggled with "whether education is more concerned with intellectual or with moral virtue" (McKeon, 1941, p. 1296). His considered judgment was that educators should develop intellectual virtues by direct instruction and foster moral virtues by instilling good habits

This duality of purpose and methods made its way into the charters of most American colleges founded prior to the late nineteenth century. Harvard's charter of 1650 called for educating youth in both knowledge and "godliness" (Hofstadter and Smith, 1961, p. 10); Brown's charter of 1764 demanded that "above all, a constant regard be paid to, and effectual care taken of, the morals of the college" (p. 33). Public universities often included similar language in their founding documents. The College of William and Mary's charter of 1693 spoke of educating youth in "good Letters and Manners" (p. 136) and the University of Georgia's charter of 1785 specifically called for instruction that would mold students "to the love of virtue and good order" (p. 151).

NEW DIRECTIONS FOR INSTITUTIONAL RESEARCH, no. 122, Summer 2004   © Wiley Periodicals, Inc.

Character Development's Rough Ride

Notwithstanding the noble intentions expressed in such documents, college faculty and presidents quickly learned that developing students' character was far more problematic than instructing them in varied intellectual subjects. Elaborate disciplinary codes and constant vigilance were insufficient to transform immature students into responsible adults. The custom of having the president teach seniors a course in moral philosophy persisted well into the nineteenth century, but there is little evidence that it added appreciably to the goal of forming students' character. Indeed, most presidents and professors felt burdened beyond relief by the expectation that they were to guard the morals and elevate the behavior of college students. Charles F. Thwing (1878), long-time president of Western Reserve University, observed that character formation was most difficult in urban colleges, where the evils of liquor, sexual opportunity, and sundry other temptations simply overpowered the exhortations of faculty. He estimated that as many as three-fifths of all undergraduates were addicted to alcohol. Isaac Sharpless, president of Haverford College, summed up the prevailing view of presidents when he wrote that "the question of discipline has always occupied a large, and not infrequently the largest, place in college life" (1915, p. 135).

Extensive attention was given to discipline both because it was practically necessary to educational operations given the young age of most students and because it was thought to fulfill colleges' commitment to character formation. Rigid discipline helped to maintain order in the classroom and residence hall and on the college grounds. It also limited town-gown rowdiness and curtailed students' natural inclination to bring noncollege friends to campus. College officials deemed maintenance of discipline an essential component of their educational responsibility since by instilling proper habits of behavior they assumed that good character would follow.

Corporate and civic leaders were not much impressed by the latter claim. Richard T. Crane, a Chicago industrialist and philanthropist, privately printed a 331-page study in which he concluded that no collegiate claim was more absurd than that "college is a great place for the development and improvement of character" (1909, p. 121). He found the opposite to be true: that college students thought themselves privileged and outside the norms of commonly expected public behavior. He found the average college graduate less well behaved than the average young adult who had spent the same four years working for a living.

During the later decades of the nineteenth century and the early decades of the twentieth, several emerging forces exacerbated the already uneasy balance between intellectual advancement and character development on the college campus. Industrialization's focus on efficiency accelerated criticism of the classical curriculum. Professionalism encouraged narrow specialization, especially in graduate school. A growing emphasis on scientific method diminished the status of theology and altered the scholarly methods of the humanities. Creation of national scholarly societies helped to shift professors' sense of identity away from the limited sphere of their own campus. Importation of the German university model and implementation of elective systems led to compartmentalization of the curriculum, with the consequent effect of undermining the appeal of a consistent program of study for all students. Moreover, the sheer growth of enrollment in many institutions challenged presidents and faculty to maintain traditional practices and procedures. In the larger institutions bureaucracy flourished, and with it came diminished personal attention. After World War II, an influx of adult, international, and part-time students compounded the difficulties campuses faced in developing students' character. There seemed to be too many variations in interests, schedules, needs, and backgrounds to address. Many institutions added programs and services and still lost ground in terms of effectively maintaining personal contact with each student.

These social and educational trends did not swiftly or entirely replace the old-time college with a new university model but instead stirred what historian Laurence Veysey (1965, p. vii) termed a "most striking . . . diversity of mind" among educators. Defenders of the older rubric fought hard to maintain traditional liberal arts colleges with their attention to character development. Others touted the new freedoms and socially useful features of universities and technical schools, where advancement of knowledge and professional practice could flower. The lines were not drawn tightly, however. Many colleges selectively adopted curricular reforms pioneered by universities, and some university presidents continued to argue for character development as an important aim of all higher learning.

Perhaps the most profound impact of these trends was on the *manner* in which character development came to be fostered by institutions of higher learning. If the old approach could be defined by the notion that pervasive collegiate disciplinary rules were to enforce good habits, which in turn would shape personal character, then the newer approach assumed that students should take primary responsibility for their own morals and behavior, on the basis of enlightened views acquired from the ordinary college curriculum (Wagoner, 1968). In the words of Stanford University's founding president, David Starr Jordan (1896, p. 72), a student's "character he must form for himself; but higher education gives him the materials." *In loco parentis* lost favor as the twentieth century unfolded, leaving most campuses with minimal disciplinary codes and most mission statements with only shadowy expectations regarding character development.

By the late 1950s, scholars and critics at large were beginning to voice concerns about the minimal impact of higher education on morals, values, and character. Philip E. Jacob published a controversial review of research on the subject and concluded that "the weight of evidence indicates that actually very little change occurs during college in the essential standards by which students govern their lives" (1957, p. 53). Two years later Edward D. Eddy, Jr., provost of the University of New Hampshire, published *The College Influence on Student Character* (1959) under the auspices of the American Council on Education. Eddy argued that character development was too important to be ignored by colleges, although he admitted that institutions under different auspices would need to take different approaches. In general, he criticized colleges for taking too much for granted, for being rigid and uncreative in their methods, and for failing to develop comprehensive programs of character development. The civic turbulence of the following decade broke down most remaining vestiges of character development at the larger institutions and many of the smaller ones.

By the early 1970s, William J. Jellima, research director of the Association of American Colleges, was dismayed to find on campuses "a virtual absence of concern for moral values" (Averill and Jellima, 1971, p. 137). Not much has changed during the third of a century since. The most recent study, conducted by staff of the Carnegie Foundation for the Advancement of Teaching, found that "most colleges and universities have few programs that specifically address the moral and civic development of their students, and a great many students make it all the way through college without participating in any of those programs" (Colby, Ehrlich, Beaumont, and Stephens, 2002, p. 26).

This cursory historical review is meant neither to capture the complex development of American higher education nor to imply that there was unanimity of opinion or practice in any one era or type of institution, but rather to illustrate the deep roots of our present-day ambivalence about character development. By the closing decades of the twentieth century, a majority of American colleges and universities had marginalized or removed character development as an explicit educational goal. Only in rare instances did a president, board, or faculty senate publicly declare character development to be irrelevant or undesirable. Most simply drifted over time into a frame of reference in which intellectualism, secularism, professionalism, and individualism were deemed central; character development, though laudable, no longer seemed to be an achievable or publicly expected goal of higher education.

Today the typical college or university mission statement speaks at best obliquely about institutional responsibility for character development. Harvard mentions only encouraging "responsibility for the consequences of personal actions" and Brown speaks vaguely of "preparing students to discharge the offices of life with usefulness and reputation." The College of William and Mary hopes to instill in students "an appreciation for the human condition, a concern for the public well-being," while the University of Georgia promises to promote "cultural, ethnic, racial, and gender diversity" and "the ideals of an open, democratic society." These formulations are notably limited compared to the goals stated in their founding charters.

Voices of Support for Character Development

The tradition of explicit attention to character development has been kept alive throughout the past half-century primarily by a subset of liberal arts colleges, military academies, and religiously affiliated colleges and universities. For example, Earlham College's mission statement stresses "high moral standards of personal conduct," and Ithaca College dedicates itself "to fostering intellectual growth, aesthetic appreciation, and character development." Roberts Wesleyan College aims to develop "moral and religious culture, correct principles and good character, personal piety and social action." The U.S. Military Academy at West Point designs its programs to ensure that "each graduate is a commissioned leader of character." Stonehill College is committed to developing "emotional growth" and "personal responsibility." Loyola University in Chicago "encourages students to develop all dimensions of themselves—intellectual, emotional, physical, creative, moral, and spiritual."

Although institutions such as these seem to have cornered the market on character development during the better part of the past century, a small group of presidents from research universities and secular colleges has publicly called upon other institutions of higher education to invest more effort in developing students' values, ethics, civic behavior, or character. My personal perspective as a former university president is that most of these exhortations had minimal immediate impact, since at most institutions there were (and still are) too many entrenched practices and forces to permit readily adding new (or renewed) goals to a university's mission. Yet there are signs of hope. During the most recent years, in particular, more curricular and co-curricular experiments are being tried. Voices in favor of some form of character development seem to be growing in number, and methods of assessing college outcomes are improving in sophistication. For those new to the discussion, a sampling of such presidential statements from the past twenty years may be helpful.

In 1984, President James T. Laney of Emory University wrote an article on presidential leadership in which he observed "a yearning in the higher education community for an appreciation and cultivation of the moral dimension" (p. 19). He found, however, that faculty took little interest in dealing with students' morals or behavior, especially outside the classroom. It seemed to him that the academy "simply abandoned" students after class. In contrast, Laney argued, somewhat guardedly, that "education should not merely confer competence, it should also shape character" (p. 19). He recommended that presidents take the lead.

A few years later, president Derek Bok of Harvard issued a stirring call for universities to improve the moral and ethical education of their students. He reported that highly publicized ethical lapses by Jim Bakker, Ivan Boesky, Michael Deaver, and Oliver North had created a national concern about prevailing moral values, especially among the most educated. College courses in ethics, though increasingly numerous, were seldom well taught and were based on the questionable premise that moral reasoning was sufficient to produce ethical behavior. He concluded that "despite the importance of moral development to the individual student and the society, one cannot say that higher education has demonstrated a deep concern for the problem" (Bok, 1988, p. 50). Bok called upon faculties to supplement general courses in ethics with specialized courses in applied ethics and with opportunities throughout the curriculum to discuss moral issues. He also urged more just campus policies, replete with explanation of their underlying values. He recommended expansion of community service projects and an enriched campus environment that would teach by habit, example, and exhortation without becoming dependent upon particular religious doctrines. He called specifically upon presidents and deans to lead the way, noting in closing that "students must get help from their universities in developing moral standards or they are unlikely to get much assistance at all" (p. 50).

In 1993, the Johnson Foundation convened sixteen leaders, among them six college and university presidents, to examine the question, "What does society need from higher education?" Their report posited "a disturbing and dangerous mismatch" between what society needed and what American higher education was delivering. The first of their three major findings was that institutions of higher learning were "enmeshed in, and in some ways contributing to, society's larger crisis of values" by failing to transmit "an understanding of good and bad, right and wrong, and the compelling core values any society needs to sustain itself" (Wingspread Group on Higher Education, 1993, p. 4). The Wingspread Group called upon colleges and universities to reaffirm the conviction that "the moral purpose of knowledge is at least as important as its utility" (p. 7).

The kinds of moral values the Wingspread Group had in mind were not derived from any particular religious creed but instead from Constitutional language and national experience, including "the belief that our common interests exceed our individual differences," "concern for those who come after us," "respect for the views of others," "the belief that individual rights and privileges are to be exercised responsibly," and "the conviction that no one is above the law" (p. 9). Institutions of higher education were called upon to ensure that entering freshmen would graduate "as individuals of character more sensitive to the needs of the community, more competent in their ability to contribute to society, and more civil in their habits of thought, speech, and action" (p. 9). The Wingspread Group offered a self-assessment instrument for institutions to use in evaluating their own performance as well as practical suggestions for improving character formation. They included collaborative learning, community service, experiential learning, and direct discussion of moral issues. The moral questions raised on a campus might be deeply troubling, the report conceded, but the Wingspread participants believed this discomfort would be a sign that important values were being addressed.

Five years after the Wingspread meeting, another select group of university presidents and distinguished international leaders met in Glion, Switzerland, to discuss the challenges facing higher education globally. Frank T. Rhodes, president emeritus of Cornell University, published the collective views of the group in the form of *The Glion Declaration: The University at the Millennium*. Although the group did not explicitly call for universities to engage in character development, it affirmed that teaching is a moral vocation, with "the goal of producing not only highly skilled, but also broadly educated, self-motivated graduates who have a thirst for lifelong learning, are aware of their heritage, are conscious of their civic obligations, and are ethically responsible in their professional careers" (Association of Governing Boards, 1998, p. 5). No advice was offered about how to foster these outcomes.

A year later, President Harold Shapiro of Princeton University (1999) enjoined the issue by observing a continued increase in public concern "over the lack of principled and responsible behavior in both public and private life." The addition of "private life" is notable, since most presidents of large institutions then and now restrict their comments to the on-campus or civic aspects of students' behavior. Shapiro called upon universities to give students' lives moral significance, acknowledging that "complex moral reasoning is not a substitute for moral behavior." Although admitting that the task is daunting and cannot be addressed by adopting the discarded practices of prior generations, he concluded that universities should not abdicate this responsibility to others.

In the same year, President James W. Abbott of the University of South Dakota and his vice president, Donald C. Dahlin, published a brief article advocating that universities go beyond the "'soft form' of in loco parentis" provided by student life offices on campus. General education programs in our universities, they said, "must continue to be concerned about our students' character development" (Dahlin and Abbott, 1999, p. 207). Yet they cautioned that powerful forces would need to be overcome for this to happen, including a softening of discipline-centered curricula and deconstructionist influences. They also acknowledged that the credit-hour system constitutes a barrier to translating lofty goals into effective curricula.

College and university presidents are not the only leaders to express opinions about the role of higher education in developing character. Civic leaders, foundation executives, and corporate CEOs have also called upon the nation's universities and colleges to do a better job of educating a more civic-minded citizenry and a more ethical workforce. For instance, David Mathews, former Secretary of Health, Education, and Welfare in the Ford Administration and later president of the Charles F. Kettering Foundation, asked "why should anyone—other than family members, close friends, and perhaps immediate neighbors—care about my, or for that matter, *your* character?" (Mathews, 1997, p. 11). His answer was that we all share a common fate and that the "civic character" of educated individuals will determine our future as a nation. In an era when voting is declining, civic institutions are losing legitimacy, and society is becoming progressively more adversarial and individualistic, it is increasingly critical that college students learn about, experience, and reflect upon civic virtues.

When recently the National Urban League interviewed two hundred corporate executives from Fortune 1000 companies to ask what traits and attributes of business leaders best foster success, the finding was that "character—defined as integrity, determination, grit—is the most crucial quality" (National Urban League, 2001, p. 2). Character, they said, was more important than leadership, motivation, communication skills, or personality traits. One-third of the CEOs interviewed stated that character was the sole criterion used in promoting individuals to senior positions within their company. This finding assumes, of course, that individuals under consideration already possessed the necessary technical competence. Nonetheless, it is noteworthy that character (even in the limited definition of this study) is deemed to be such a salient quality of success at the highest levels of corporate leadership.

Perhaps the most striking element of the National Urban League report is that it contradicts a long-developing pattern reported by Stephen R. Covey in his 1989 national bestseller, *The 7 Habits of Highly Effective People*. Covey observed a twentieth-century shift away from the "character ethic" that had defined leadership during the first 150 years of our nation. In its place had arisen a "personality ethic," in which image became more important than attitudes or values. Even so, in the National Urban League study character was at the top of the list of valued attributes and personality at the bottom. Whether this shift represents an artifact of the study methods or a genuine change in leadership expectations remains to be seen, but at the very least it signals an opportunity for institutions of higher learning to seek partnership with sympathetic corporate leaders.

Scholars who study effective and ineffective leaders have often reported that character is a key to success. Warren Bennis, who spent decades observing and interviewing leaders and board members, stated simply that "leadership is character" (1997, p. 72). By this he meant that good leadership depends more upon integrity and moral fabric than upon image or mere intellectual ability. The reason, he explained, is that leaders "set the tone for the moral character, vision, culture, and the fiber of the institution" (p. 179). The other two critical elements of leadership success, according to Bennis, are expertise and ambition.

James M. Kouzes and Barry Z. Posner also conducted national studies of leadership traits and concluded that both leaders and their colleagues value honesty as the most desirable characteristic a leader can possess (1993). Other highly valued character traits were cooperativeness, fair-mindedness, and dependability. However, a disheartening aspect of contemporary leadership is that reality so often falls far short of what is desired. Kouzes and Posner reported that in one major U.S. corporation 87 percent of office workers considered it "very important" that management be "honest, upright, and ethical," yet only 40 percent said this statement was "very true" in their own work setting (p. 35). Since these studies were completed, our economy has been shaken and humiliated by high-profile ethical lapses in government, the accounting industry, the Catholic Church, professional sports, banks and brokerage houses, and corporations such as Enron and WorldCom. There seems to be a growing public consensus, however fragile it may be in practice, that the time has come for good character to count more in civic life and corporate America.

It is beyond the scope of this chapter to estimate how extensively colleges and universities are willing to take up the task of attending to character formation, let alone whether they are capable of making a significant difference. When university presidents discuss possibilities, they usually acknowledge a pervasive uneasiness at the prospect of directly engaging in character formation or moral education—except in the kinds of institutions previously noted. On the other hand, a growing number of presidents, deans, and faculty members are supporting curricular and co-curricular initiatives that *affect* students' character in a helpful way. Spurred by such organizations as Campus Compact, the Association of American Colleges and Universities, the Lilly Endowment, and the Templeton Foundation, institutions are increasingly engaging undergraduate students in activities within and outside the classroom that bring them into personal and meaningful contact with ethical issues, moral codes, and civic responsibilities. As these institutional efforts expand and mature, both critics and supporters look to researchers to document the outcomes of programs designed in whole or part to develop character. It is here that institutional researchers will provide an essential service to educational leaders.

Research to the Rescue

One of the surest ways to encourage higher education's leaders to support undergraduate character development is to demonstrate that efforts are both effective and lacking in significant negative side effects. Presidents, like professors, are pulled in many directions. Time is scarce and financial resources are too limited to satisfactorily address the other priorities already identified. Moreover, matters of ethics, morals, and personal responsibility are a lightning rod in our culture, quickly evoking passion in every quarter. In this climate, a call to action is likely to be accepted either because new revenue sources become available to address a compelling social problem or because there is evidence that valuable educational outcomes can be achieved without unduly imposing on existing traditions, practices, and resources. In the next sections I list some of the reasons college and university presidents and other leaders will take an increasing interest in studies that document the favorable impact of college on character development.

Character Outcomes Affect Accreditation. During the past decade, regional and specialized accreditation standards have exerted more influence than any other factor on increasing assessment of educational outcomes (John S. and James L. Knight Foundation, 2000). Regional accreditors rely upon each institution's board-approved mission statement to identify the outcomes that warrant assessment. Professional accreditors customarily do this as well, but they also evaluate institutional goals and student outcomes against a grid of competencies required by the profession. In either case, the minimum expectation is that an institution must demonstrate that its students in aggregate are achieving stated learning objectives.

Quite recent trends in accrediting standards are placing more emphasis on the relationship between the educational aims appearing in a mission statement and the specific types of outcome evidence submitted. Rarely does it suffice any longer to submit only graduation ratios, student satisfaction surveys, and alumni placement data as evidence of institutional effectiveness. Colleges and universities are being told to develop or adopt measures that directly address their stated learning goals. This is likely to mean in the domain of character development that institutions enjoying reliable data about character development during the college years will be able to retain or introduce related goals in their mission statement and institutional planning documents. Lacking such outcome data or the near-term prospect of it, presidents and boards may find it prudent to diminish the salience of, or entirely remove, goal statements concerning character development, morality, and ethics.

Character Outcomes Can Help Recruit Students. If there has been one pervasive trend in methods of recruiting students during the past quarter-century, it is the adoption of commercial marketing practices. Admissions officers were replaced by enrollment managers, who now are being augmented or replaced by marketing experts (internal or external). It is beyond the scope of this work to assess the positive and negative consequences of this trend, but it is important to note that one effect has been pronounced escalation of the rhetoric of excellence. Every college and university, no matter what its circumstances or achievements, claims to be an institution of excellence responsive to students and producing graduates of high quality.

Amid the welter of such claims, how are prospective students and their families to know what to believe? One way an institution can gain the upper hand in the war of rhetoric is to supplement image building with data gathering. Reliable outcome data in a form comprehensible to the public make it possible for marketing efforts to focus on what a student can actually expect to take away from an institution. To the extent that published comparisons, such as the annual ratings in *U.S. News & World Report*, come to rely on outcomes measures rather than supply-side measures, the marketing advantage afforded by positive data is enhanced. Institutions that can prove they are contributing to character development and formation of civic virtue may enjoy a decided advantage in recruiting students—provided, of course, that other desired resources and outcomes also are present.

Character Outcomes Can Increase Philanthropy. Philanthropy comes in many forms, from the small annual fund check to corporate giving, foundation support, and major gifts from an institution's wealthiest alumni and friends. One trend widely observed in recent years is that donors are showing more interest in the *impact* of their generosity. A decreasing proportion of corporate and foundation giving is for general institutional support and a rising proportion is tied to specific programs, audiences, or partnerships that make a visible difference outside the walls of the campus (Lovett, 2003). Some corporate and private foundations are also altering their funding priorities to address civic weaknesses of the sort already mentioned.

Presidents, development officers, and grant officers improve their chance of success if they can furnish credible information that their institutions are effective. The claim has two components. First an institution that knows how to use the resources it already has will be effective in using new resources. The second stage of the argument is that an institution that knows how to evaluate outcomes will be both attentive to outcomes and capable of proving whether the proposed intervention is helpful. Donors appreciate honest efforts. They know that not every initiative is successful, but they want to know what succeeds, what does not, and why. An institution with a strong record of assessing outcomes places itself in a favorable competitive position. There are relatively few such institutions as of this writing.

Character Outcomes Captivate Legislators. Public funding for higher education is in disarray. Federal and state governments are hard hit by declining tax revenues, and local taxing bodies are struggling to fund basic community services. Both public and private institutions of higher learning have faced substantial budget cuts, with the prospect that more may be in the offing. In addition, federal agencies and state coordinating bodies are growing more insistent that colleges and universities demonstrate their needs, show they are cost-effective, and prove they are worthy of a past level of public funding. Such concerns often play out in regulatory demands for new and more detailed data reporting.

If university and college presidents are to make the case both to legislators and to the public at large that heavy investment in higher education continues to make sense during a period of economic turmoil—perhaps especially during such a period—they must do so in part by answering the oft-heard claim that college graduates contribute less than they should to the common good (other than by paying higher taxes based on higher personal income). Critics of higher education have long insisted that colleges and universities shirk their public duty to help form civic-minded graduates who contribute pervasively and positively to society. To the extent that out-come studies can yield evidence that such effects are occurring, a president stands a much improved chance of persuading legislators and the voting public that their support is well deserved.

Character Outcomes Make Graduates More Successful in Business. If we accept the previously cited findings of researchers to the effect that people with exemplary character are in high demand for leadership positions, then it seems safe to assume that colleges demonstrating positive changes in character during the undergraduate years will, on average, produce more successful graduates. The same logic applies to alumni who enter the professions. Some professions, notably law, already require those applying for a license to show evidence of good character (Brennan, 1989). Other professions are mindful of character considerations even though they do not as yet have a formal screening process (Johnson and Campbell, 2002; Martin, 1999). In many other occupations as well, good character has been found to promote business success (Solomon, 1992).

Thomas Teal, former senior editor of the *Harvard Business Review*, surveyed the business landscape and concluded that "managing" has become one of the most common of all jobs. Almost everyone who has been in the workplace more than a few years seems to be managing other people or critical functions. Yet he found that little attention is paid to how a manager's character affects his or her human interactions. Teal concluded that "one reason for the scarcity of managerial greatness is that in educating and training managers, we focus too much on technical proficiency and too little on character" (1996, p. 36). It would follow, then, that colleges and universities that do both are well positioned to have successful and grateful alumni as well as employers eager to hire their graduates. Perhaps partial evidence of this is that 60 percent of the CEOs of the nation's leading corporations and 95 percent of the CEOs of the top twenty banks were educated at small liberal arts colleges (Splete, n.d., p. 8).

Character Outcomes Can Transform Campus Life. Institutions of higher education in the United States are characterized by a mutual skepticism between faculty and administration. Presidents often are heard to say, "Well, I like that idea, but I'm not so sure the faculty will go along with it." Faculty in turn generally feel overburdened and insufficiently supported with regard to responsibilities they already have. The prospect of undertaking new or enlarged responsibilities suggested by someone else usually elicits a response on the order of "not unless they give me release time, an assistant, and some added money in the budget." Faculty have been especially resistant to accept responsibility for developing students' moral character, personal values, or emotional stability (Trice and Dey, 1997). Philip Stone (2000), president of Bridgewater College, found that some faculty are skeptical about the appropriateness of this role, while others feel they lack proper training or are reluctant to confront issues that are personally troubling.

However, success breeds interest, and it is here that good outcome data can be of help. If initial interventions aimed at developing student character can be shown to be effective, then faculty may be more inclined to experiment further and campus administrators will be more willing to allocate resources. Success breeds more success. Even failure can breed success. If outcome data demonstrate significant deficiencies, especially on nationally normed measures, campuses are prone to respond more quickly than they otherwise would. The threat of poor publicity is a powerful motivator.

Two other ways in which successful efforts at character development can help to transform campus life are through an altered campus ethos and by students' acting in a more mature manner. Campuses carrying out the best work in character development do so comprehensively by changing curricula, campus policies, co-curricular services, hiring and promotion criteria, disciplinary practices, and a host of other campus features. In so doing, they literally transform the institution for employees, alumni, and visitors—not just for students. In consciously modeling good character for students, faculty and administrative staff improve how they themselves relate to one another. This is a topic on which additional research would be welcome.

Perhaps most important of all, campuses that focus comprehensively on character development have a better probability of effectively redressing a range of ethical and moral issues that infest student life: academic dishonesty, date rape, alcohol and substance abuse, bigotry and intolerance, theft, sexual harassment, chronic irresponsibility. Although most student life professionals on campus now see their primary responsibility as promoting learning rather than shaping behavior, both of their professional organizations (ACPA and NASPA) post on their Web sites seven principles of good practice, among them helping students "develop coherent values and ethical standards." By this they mean fostering "justice, honesty, equality, civility, freedom, dignity, and responsible citizenship." The cause is worthy. As Nannerl Keohane, president of Duke University, noted (1999, p. 2), research shows that "campus norms and practice . . . can make a significant difference in student behaviors, attitudes, and beliefs."

Character Outcomes Confer Bragging Rights. Presidents are not alone in representing the public image of their campus, but certainly they are called upon constantly to speak well about their institution. In a typical day a president may be asked to address business leaders, a donor prospect, a scholarly assembly or visiting dignitary, a group of alumni, prospective students or employees, and perhaps a disgruntled parent. In every one of these situations, and many others that make up the life of a president, it is helpful to have reliable information ready to demonstrate the institution's achievements.

In public settings where a president is expected to promote his or her institution, having bragging rights is highly prized. Often stories of stellar performance by a student or faculty member form the basis of a president's remarks. Fortunate is the president with good statistics who can say "on this national measure of performance, we are in the top 5 percent" (or better). Even in one-on-one discussion, a president can make use of positive outcome data. Whether it be in attempting to lure a promising prospect to join the campus community or in dealing with a failing student who is blaming the institution for his or her academic shortcomings, the president (or other campus official) who is armed with positive outcome data can respond encouragingly by saying "This is the way we do it here, and here is why we know our methods really work." Once again, proof of success is a powerful motivator.

Character Outcomes Can Improve President-Board Relations. The tenure of a president is notoriously short. Presidents come into office full of energy and ideas, eager to work with all campus constituencies, and believing that they will lead a golden era of reform. Most are educators at heart, anxious to make life better for students and faculty. Some succeed brilliantly, but many do not—hence, short tenure. Mounting stresses burn out a president quickly, and often budgetary or other crises either lead to a president's departure or force him or her to devote an unsatisfying degree of attention to just a few issues. With the rush of people and decisions that face a president every day, fatigue and frustration become a corollary of overwork, even when things are going well.

Outcome data are useful to presidents for all of the reasons enumerated here, but they may be especially useful in dealing with the board of trustees. Almost all presidents serve at the pleasure of a board. As Clark Kerr long ago reminded us, boards hire and remove presidents "with enthusiasm." In between, they tend to want a continuous record of achievement. Since a president routinely must come to the board with budget requests, building plans, and visions for a bold new future, the board understandably looks for evidence of success to date. Presidents who can demonstrate positive outcomes from current programs enjoy a basis of credibility that greatly enhances their persuasive ability.

Presidents, like professors, labor in a vineyard where most of the grapes are hard to see or taste. So much of the difficult work done on a campus bears fruit only years later. On occasion, grateful alumni or employers think to call a professor or president to express their gratitude for providing a fine education, but in general the academic seasons roll by with one cohort of new faces replacing the prior one. Presidents (and for that matter, most staff and faculty) take pride in what they do, and they look for evidence of achievement. Perhaps this is one reason faculty take so much pleasure in seeking grants, getting published, and winning honors—the results of effort are known and, when favorable, are publicized. So it can be with measures of student learning. A campus that produces positive change in students can take greater pride in its work and become better known for what it does. A president who leads this type of institution will enjoy the rewards of success too, in lengthened tenure, improved compensation, and a greater sense of self-satisfaction. Character outcomes are only one facet of institutional achievement, but I suspect that most presidents and board members take a keener-than-average interest in evidence that a campus is producing better people, not just better educated people.

Character Outcomes Improve Society. This exploration ends where it began, with the observation that citizens who are intellectually alive and morally virtuous have the most to contribute to their community and to the nation. Not only do they have the greatest ability to act for the common good, while carefully advancing their own best interests, but they also are more disposed to do so. This is perhaps the crux of the issue. Our society lacks neither technical competence nor resources of a material nature. We fail to mend our societal shortcomings because we lack the will and the force of character to do so.

In proclaiming National Character Counts Week last year, President George W. Bush opened his remarks by observing that "many of our society's most cherished values . . . depend in practice on individual character" (Bush, 2003). Assisting each new generation to develop intellectual capacity and technical skill must remain the core mission of American colleges and universities, but our institutions of higher learning also ought to contribute to the formation of citizens who embody the common virtues embraced by all civilized societies. Integrity, justice, fairness, tolerance, compassion, cooperation, and prudence *can* be shaped to some degree during the college years. It may not be easy to do so, and many of our institutions have forgotten how to try, but there are enough successful examples to give hope to those disposed to make a greater effort.

Leaders of our colleges and universities must stand beside corporate, religious, and civic leaders in proclaiming that character makes a difference and is worth developing at every stage of the educational process. Then we must do whatever we can inside our institutions, and in cooperation with other organizations, to bring character development within the reach of our diverse student body. We can apply our research skills, pedagogical creativity, and growing community involvement in ways that effect positive, measurable changes. "The goal is not to indoctrinate students," Ernest Boyer reminds us, "but to set them free in a world of ideas and provide a *climate* in which ethical and moral choices can be thoughtfully examined, and convictions formed" (Boyer, 1987, p. 284, emphasis added).

References

Association of Governing Boards. *The Glion Declaration: The University at the Millennium.* Washington, D.C.: Association of Governing Boards, 1998.

Averill, L. J., and Jellima, W. J. (eds.). *Colleges and Commitments.* Philadelphia: Westminster Press, 1971.

Bennis, W. *Managing People Is Like Herding Cats.* Provo, Utah: Executive Excellence, 1997.

Bok, D. "Ethics, the University, and Society." *Harvard Magazine,* 1988, *90*(5), 39–50.

Boyer, E. L. *College: The Undergraduate Experience in America.* New York: HarperCollins, 1987.

Brennan, D. C. "Defining Moral Character and Fitness." *Bar Examiner,* 1989, *58*(4), 24–30.

Bush, G. W. "National Character Counts Week, 2003." Presidential proclamation, Oct. 20, 2003.

Colby, A., Ehrlich, T., Beaumont, E., and Stephens, J. "Moral and Civic Engagement During College." *Peer Review,* 2002, *4*(4), 23–26.

Covey, S. R. *The 7 Habits of Highly Effective People.* New York: Simon & Schuster, 1989.

Crane, R. T. *The Utility of All Kinds of Higher Schooling.* Chicago: privately printed, 1909.

Dahlin, D. C., and Abbott, J. W. "Character and Undergraduate Education." *Education,* 1999, *120*(2), 204–207.

Eddy, E. D., Jr. *The College Influence on Student Character.* Washington, D.C.: American Council on Education, 1959.

Hofstadter, R., and Smith, W. (eds.). *American Higher Education: A Documentary History.* Chicago: University of Chicago Press, 1961.

Jacob, P. E. *Changing Values in College: An Exploratory Study of the Impact of College Teaching.* New York: HarperCollins, 1957.

John S. and James L. Knight Foundation. "Disputed Territories." *Policy Perspectives,* 2000, *9*(4), 1–8.

Johnson, W. B., and Campbell, C. D. "Character and Fitness Requirements for Professional Psychologists: Are There Any?" *Professional Psychology: Research and Practice,* 2002, *33*(1), 46–53.

Jordan, D. S. *The Care and Culture of Men.* San Francisco: Whitaker and Ray, 1896.

Keohane, N. O. "The Fundamental Values of Academic Integrity." Durham, N.C.: Center for Academic Integrity, Duke University, 1999.

Kouzes, J. M., and Posner, B. Z. *Credibility.* San Francisco: Jossey-Bass, 1993.

Laney, J. T. "The Moral Authority of the College or University President." *Educational Record,* 1984, *65*(2), 17–19.

Lovett, C. "Letter from the President." American Association for Higher Education, Nov. 20, 2003.

Martin, M. W. "Moral Fitness for Professions." *Perspectives on the Professions,* 1999, *18*(2), 8–9.

Mathews, D. "Character for What? Higher Education and Public Life." *Educational Record,* 1997, *78*(3–4), 10–17.

McKeon, R. (ed.). *The Basic Works of Aristotle.* New York: Random House, 1941.

National Urban League. *Spotting Talent and Potential in the Business World: Lessons from Corporate America for College Admissions.* New York: National Urban League, 2001.

Shapiro, H. T. "Liberal Education, Moral Education." *Princeton Alumni Weekly,* Jan. 27, 1999, pp. 16–21.

Sharpless, I. *The American College.* New York: Doubleday, Page, 1915.

Solomon, R. C. *Ethics and Excellence: Cooperation and Integrity in Business.* New York: Oxford University Press, 1992.

Splete, A. P. "Small by Choice: The Advantages of Small Colleges." Washington, D.C.: Council of Independent Colleges (n.d.).

Stone, P. C. "Developing the Whole Student." *New Agenda Series,* 2000, *2*(2), 75–79.

Teal, T. "The Human Side of Management." *Harvard Business Review,* 1996, *74*(6), 35–43.

Thwing, C. F. *American Colleges: Their Students and Work.* New York: Putnam, 1878.

Trice, A. G., and Dey, E. L. "Trends in Faculty Teaching Goals: A Longitudinal Study of Change." *Journal of College Student Development,* 1997, *38*(5), 527–534.

Veysey, L. R. *The Emergence of the American University.* Chicago: University of Chicago Press, 1965.

Wagoner, J. L., Jr. "From *In Loco Parentis* Toward *Lernfreiheit:* An Examination of the Attitudes of Four Early College Presidents Regarding Student Freedom and Character Development." Unpublished doctoral dissertation, Ohio State University, 1968.

Wingspread Group on Higher Education. *An American Imperative: Higher Expectations for Higher Education.* Racine, Wis.: Johnson Foundation, 1993.

RICHARD YANIKOSKI is president emeritus of Saint Xavier University, Chicago.

3

This chapter addresses the role of character development in the college experience, the dimensions that constitute it, and various methods to assess its outcomes.

Measuring Up: Defining and Assessing Outcomes of Character in College

C. Carney Strange

A focus on character development in American higher education blends well with current discussions of the place of values, civility, service, ethics, social justice, and integrity (Wingspread Group on Higher Education, 1993) in the mix of desirable ends of the college experience. So it should, since character as a construct draws from the same wellspring as these other outcomes, inasmuch as they all reflect a fundamental concern for what is valued and considered good. However, the appropriateness of these educational goals has not always enjoyed elevated status in the academy. In fact, throughout much of the history of postsecondary education their treatment has often reflected a deep divide between claims of truth (that is, knowledge) and claims of goodness (value) that has led, in the worst of times, to warring camps of righteous proponents and, in the best of times, to an uncomfortable truce among educators and citizens. Perhaps it is understood best as an on-again-off-again relationship between knowing and valuing in higher education.

To borrow labels from Huston Smith's analysis (2001) of the role of religion for individuals and society across the ages, it is helpful to think of three eras, or phases, in this relationship between knowing and valuing in the academy. The first phase is traditional, the second modern, and the third postmodern. Each phase offers its own story that shaped what was done then and shapes what we do now with questions about values, knowledge, and character in the context of higher education.

The parlance of character development in the traditional era of the colonial colleges reads much like a quaint old volume in considering its role in the formation of early proponents. These were institutions (for example, Harvard, Princeton, Yale, William and Mary) founded on a clear sense of mission: to train the leaders of a new polity demanding vision and respect for the culture and traditions of a civil society. In these institutions, attention given to the whole student entailed immersion in the values of an "established middle class, a commitment to European learning, and a Christian conception of character and culture" (Hacker, 1986, p. 5). As one author concluded, "The early American college did not doubt its responsibility to educate the whole person—body, mind, and spirit; head, heart, and hands" (Boyer, 1987, p. 177). Graduates were expected to demonstrate the best of "gentlemen" traits and a proper training embedded exclusively in the classics of Western thought. In one such early formulation, Harvard College set forth its requirements for a bachelor's degree in its laws of 1642–1650: "Every scholar that on proofe is found able to read the originall of the old and New testament into the Latin toungue, and to Resolve them Logically withall being of honest life and conversation and at any publicke act hath the approbation of the overseers, and master of the College may bee invested with his first degree" (Colonial Society of Massachusetts, *Collections,* vol. 15, pp. 26–27, as cited in Brubacher and Rudy, 1976). If not directly, the blend of understanding and character in this statement suggests that goodness and truth were one and the same in this conception of the educated person. He (mostly) was conversant in both, since what was "true" and what was "good" came from the same source. For American higher education, this traditional story lasted well into the middle of the nineteenth century.

With the advent of the land-grant university (Eddy, 1957) in the mid-1800s there emerged, in full expression, a much different and modern story, one that applauded the seeming divorce between knowing (that is, truth) and valuing (goodness), in the name of a positivistic science dedicated to building a great new edifice of method and thought. Higher education soon became a world where values and related questions were seen as irrelevant and inherently suspect, and objectivity (or the presumed freedom from values) became the principal metric of any claim to know. The concern for values and character development were slowly relegated to other institutions, while faculty newly trained in the German universities set about to discover the world through an empiricism that sought facts and theories rather than philosophies and commitments. Out of this, it was anticipated, would come the universal laws of nature that fully explained all phenomena. Questions of value and other related concerns were a source of subjectivity, bent on bias and distortion. If truth was to prevail, they must be controlled. This modern story proved the dominant one until well into the twentieth century (and in many ways, some would claim, it still does), when a new and postmodern version (Bloland, 1995) began to assert itself.

In the current postmodern story, knowing and valuing have reconciled once again, but for quite different reasons from those that sustained their union in the traditional story. Rather than value equating to truth, in this era claims of truth are increasingly exposed as an extension of exclusive values orientations. Claims to know are inherently value-laden and argu-ably a function of the power exerted by those in control. There are no grand narratives, no patterns, and no universals; there are only variations and dif-ferences of meaning and experience embedded in various hegemonies of privilege. In such a story, the meaning and relevance of scientific facts depends fundamentally on scientific paradigms. Objectivity is just another source of subjectivity.

The postmodern story comforts some in the belief that everything is valued, but others are disquieted by the realization that nothing is valued. Some celebrate the dispersion of worldviews that totalize and marginalize; others bemoan the loss of traditional cultural maps to guide us through a complex and confusing world. These concerns have become a touchstone for a number of questions circulating through the academy today: What purposes do (or should) we serve in higher education? What outcomes can our publics expect for their investment in our efforts? Aren't questions of goodness and value at least as important as questions of truth? Such probes shape the current call to attend to the values and character, at least as much as the intellect, of those who enroll in our institutions. Numerous reports and events have generated a sense of urgency in the importance of doing so, and for good reason. From various frauds perpetrated in the corporate world (for example, Enron), scandals uncovered in high political circles (Whitewater), and ethical transgressions revealed within the very bastions of honor and duty (the U.S. military academies) has come an uneasy sense that questions of character and value may have lost their footing in our cul-ture and that immediate steps need to be taken to restore this critical con-versation in the academy.

A Crisis of Value and Character

Recent reviews of American higher education have suggested that our col-leges and universities may be failing in their responsibility to prepare gradu-ates to assume the role of contributing citizen when they ignore questions of character and values in the undergraduate curriculum (Kellogg Commis-sion on the Future of State and Land-Grant Universities, 2001; Wingspread Group on Higher Education, 1993). For example, the authors of *An American Imperative: Higher Expectations for Higher Education* are quite direct and urgent in their resolution of this apparent shortcoming: "Every institution of higher education should ask itself—*now*—what it proposes to do to assure that next year's entering students will graduate as individuals of character more sensitive to the needs of community, more competent in their ability to contribute to society, and more civil in their habits of thought, speech, and action" (Wingspread Group on Higher Education, 1993, p. 9). The empha-sis on higher education's role in preparing citizens is also pivotal in another report by the National Association of State Universities and Land-Grant Colleges (Kellogg Commission, 2000), wherein the authors concluded, "We will not consider our institutions successful unless they prepare students for active participation and leadership in democratic life" (p. 24).

Among those who have championed such views, the late U.S. commissioner of education and head of the Carnegie Foundation for the Advancement of Teaching, Ernest Boyer, ended an important analysis of the undergraduate experience in American higher education with a telling conclusion and a series of poignant questions:

> In the end, the quality of the undergraduate experience is to be measured by the willingness of graduates to be socially and civically engaged. Reinhold Niebuhr once wrote, "Man cannot behold except he be committed. He cannot find himself without finding a center beyond himself." The idealism of the undergraduate experience must reflect itself in loyalties that transcend self. Is it too much to expect that, even in this hard-edged, competitive age, a college graduate will live with integrity, civility—even compassion? Is it appropriate to hope that the lessons learned in a liberal education will reveal themselves in the humaneness of the graduate's relationship with others? [1987, pp. 278–279]

Boyer's emphasis on the communal aspects of living and learning on campus is critical to the kind of world educators are trying to shape. He reiterated: "We emphasize this commitment to community not out of a sentimental attachment to tradition, but because our democratic way of life and perhaps our survival as a people rest on whether we can move beyond self-interest and begin to understand better the realities of our dependence on each other" (p. 8). Finally, he concluded his analysis with an eye toward public purposes: "We more comfortably embrace the notion that the aim of the undergraduate experience is not only to prepare the young for productive careers, but also to enable them to live lives of dignity and purpose; not only to generate new knowledge, but to channel that knowledge to humane ends; not merely to study government, but to help shape a citizenry that can promote the public good" (p. 297).

Such aims seem to square up well with the goals most often cited in the current discussion of values and character development in education.

Defining Character

Growing interest in the nature of character and influences on character development has generated many insights and schemas for articulating this concept, as well as for guiding its measurement and implementation. The construct of character has been defined variously in the literature, sometimes focusing on the components and structures of moral reasoning and functioning (for example, Berkowitz and Fekula, 1999; Gilligan, 1982; Kohlberg, 1969; Rest, 1979), sometimes measuring the character-related behavioral outcomes of various educational interventions (for example,

Astin and Antonio, 2000), and other times identifying those admirable traits and virtues marking persons of good repute (for example, Lickona, 1998; Seligman, 1998).

Longest standing in the discussions of character in the academy have been the contributions of those mapping the developmental structures of moral reasoning and functioning. Kohlberg's seminal work, articulating a sequence of purported stages individuals proceed through as they weigh moral choices within a social system of justice, is perhaps most familiar to observers in this domain. Through the lens of women's experiences, Gilligan (1982) also has contributed to an understanding of character development as a progression of increasingly complex reasoning structures that negotiate moral choices through an ethic of care. The advanced form in both models equates to a development of character, in that each is framed and motivated by the highest principles, fidelity to universal justice and fairness in the former and commitment to nonviolence in the latter.

Another perspective on character comes from those who focus on the individual's behavior within a social context. Astin and Antonio (2000), for example, have defined character as "the values and behavior . . . reflected in the ways we interact with each other and in the moral choices we make on a daily basis" (p. 4). The outcomes they identified as prevalent in the character development literature are civic responsibility, cultural awareness and sensitivity, volunteerism, importance of raising a family, religious beliefs and convictions, and understanding of others. These outcomes are also reflective of the criteria used by the Templeton Foundation in determining which schools to honor in its assessment of "institutions of character." Similarly, Berkowitz and Fekula (1999) have discussed such development in terms of the "growth of an individual's capacity to function as an effective moral agent" (p. 18). Accordingly, they endorse the Character Education Partnership definition of character as "knowing, caring about and acting upon core ethical values such as caring, honesty, fairness, responsibility, and respect for self and others" (p. 18). Isaacs (1976) created a developmental scheme of twenty-four virtues, grouped according to the age at which they should be emphasized (for example, obedience is prominent up to seven years of age, and optimism from sixteen to eighteen), and DeMarco (1996) recommended twenty-eight virtues in his model of character. Lickona (1998) drew on the cognitive, affective, and behavioral aspects of morality to connect "moral knowing, moral feeling, and moral action. Good character," he suggests, "consists of knowing the good, desiring the good, and doing the good—habits of the mind, habits of the heart, and habits of behavior" (p. 2).

A third perspective on this topic comes from a line of inquiry that attempts to identify, define, and measure the traits and qualities of human character. For example, from the "empirical study of flourishing individuals and thriving communities" (Seligman, 1998) has emerged an interest in "positive psychology." According to Pawelski (2003), one of the central missions of this rapidly expanding branch of psychology is the "development of an operationalized classification of the strengths and virtues that constitute character." To this end, a pair of recent volumes—the *Values in Action (VIA) Classification of Strengths Manual* (Peterson and Seligman, 2003) and *Positive Psychological Assessment: A Handbook of Models and Measures* (Lopez and Snyder, 2003)—have pursued the challenge of identifying the "core virtues that are consistently valued across cultures and across time. . . . wisdom, courage, humanity, justice, temperance, and transcendence" (Pawelski, 2003). For positive psychologists, "good character is a function of these six virtues." Each of these six virtues is operationalized further in reference to certain qualities and capacities that make up a list of twenty-four strengths purported to be related to positive human functioning. For example, the first virtue category, *wisdom and knowledge,* includes an assessment of curiosity and interest in the world; love of learning; judgment, critical thinking, and open-mindedness; ingenuity, originality, practical intelligence, and street smarts; social, personal, and emotional intelligence; and perspective. A second category, *courage,* incorporates valor and bravery; perseverance, industry, and diligence; and integrity, genuineness, and honesty. *Humanity and love,* the third category of virtue in this schema, embraces kindness and generosity as well as loving and allowing oneself to be loved. The fourth virtue, *justice,* refers to citizenship, duty, teamwork, and loyalty; fairness and equity; and leadership. *Temperance,* the next category, includes self-control; prudence, discretion, and caution; and humility and modesty, while the sixth virtue in the model, *transcendence,* makes reference to appreciation of beauty and excellence; gratitude; hope, optimism, and future-mindedness; spirituality, sense of purpose, faith, and religiousness; forgiveness and mercy; playfulness and humor; and zest, passion, and enthusiasm. A profile of these twenty-four strengths for any given individual constitutes an assessment of his or her overall strength of character.

Such a list of strengths demonstrates not only the encompassing nature of the construct "character" but also the potentially far-reaching consequence of these qualities for the breadth of human functioning. After all, where would human progress be without wisdom and knowledge? Could the challenges of history and culture have been met without the courage of leaders? Can communities survive in the absence of humanity and love, and justice? From where would come our inspiration if dimensions of transcendence were ignored or lost?

In a similar manner, researchers at the U.S. Air Force Academy have constructed the concept of character in terms of twelve dimensions they assess (Barlow, Jordan, and Hendrix, 2003), but with a particular eye toward how these might contribute to the development of leaders. They are *integrity* (consistently adhering to a moral or ethical code or standard), *honesty* (being truthful with others), *loyalty* (being devoted and committed to one's organization, supervisors, coworkers, and subordinates), *selflessness* (genuine concern about the welfare of others and being willing to sacrifice one's personal interest for others and their organization), *compassion* (concern for the suffering or welfare of others and providing aid or showing mercy for others), *competency* (capable of performing tasks assigned in a superior fashion and excelling in all task assignments effectively and efficiently), *respect-fulness* (esteem for, and consideration and appreciation of, other people), *fairness* (treating people equitably, impartially, and justly), *responsibility and self-discipline* (being depended upon to make rational and logical decisions and to do tasks assigned without supervision), *decisiveness* (capable of making logical and effective decisions in a timely manner, after considering appropriate data), *spiritual appreciation* (valuing the spiritual diversity among individuals with different backgrounds and cultures and respecting all individuals' rights to differ from others in their beliefs), and *cooperativeness* (willingness to work or act together with others in accomplishing a task or some common end or purpose).

Distillation of these lists of attributes reveals a composite of qualities that frame character as a function of personal identity, including one's attitudes, values, beliefs, and abilities (such as responsibility and self-discipline); how one relates to others (for example, with cooperativeness and compassion); and toward what ends one is committed and one acts (toward transcendence and justice, for instance). To possess character is to name with confidence where one is going and how one's actions reflect that commitment, to understand how one's identity affirms such a goal, and to stand connected to others in the midst of a community that supports it.

Developing Character

With the growing interest in questions about character, numerous educational initiatives have been undertaken in attempts to systematically influence its development among students. From work within the Character Education Partnership, Berkowitz (n.d.) identified a taxonomy of character education types, each with its own focus and strategy (http://www.character.org/resources/ceppublications). They are programs with an emphasis on *moral reasoning/cognitive development,* where the discussion of moral dilemmas facilitates student development of moral reasoning capacities; *moral education/virtue,* focusing on academic content (for example, literature and history) used to teach about moral traditions in order to facilitate moral habits and internal moral qualities (virtues); *life skills education,* stressing practical skills (such as communication) and positive social attitudes (self-esteem and others); *service learning,* offering hands-on experiences of community service integrated into the curriculum; *citizenship training/civics education,* addressing specific civic values (such as leadership and participation) taught as a preparation for future citizenship; *caring community,* fostering caring relationships in various institutional settings; *health education and problem prevention,* with interventions designed to prevent unhealthy, antisocial behaviors (social norming and others); *conflict resolution/peer mediation* training programs, where students learn to mediate peer conflicts as a means of developing constructive conflict resolution skills; *ethics/moral philosophy,* examining specific ethical systems and moral philosophies; and *religious education,* taught in the context of a particular faith tradition, justifying morality from a transcendent source.

Although most of the literature on this topic addresses the challenges of character development in public education (K-12)—and though there is much to be learned from these efforts—initiatives at the postsecondary level have also received growing attention among educators recently (Blimling, 1990). Under a number of rubrics ("civic education," "values initiatives," "learning communities," "service programs," and others), an increasing number of colleges and universities have joined various national efforts (for example, Campus Compact and the Templeton Foundation) to restore a focus on opportunities for development of character as an expected outcome of higher learning. In doing so, educators (perhaps now more than ever) are reclaiming the holistic framework of teaching and learning that once served to prepare students as much for life as it did for making a living.

Among the earliest initiatives in the current era to effect character development in postsecondary education are the residential-based Intentional Democratic Community (IDC) model at the University of Connecticut (Crookston, 1974) and the Sierra Project (Whiteley, 1982) at the University of California-Irvine. The IDC program tapped the merits of civic participation in creating a community where members shared power and decision making, open communications, flexibility, and organizational and individual symbiosis. The latter project used the freshman year experience and a structured group of curricular modules to enhance students' character development, defined as their "capacity for *understanding* what is right or good in increasingly complex forms, and [their] willingness or courage to *act* on those conceptions" (Whiteley, 1982, p. 14). Since these noted earlier attempts, numerous other programs and models have been implemented on American campuses, ranging from select interventions such as creation of a student service-learning center at the University of Michigan to a well-coordinated, whole institutional transformation such as the one under way at the U.S. Air Force Academy (Berkowitz and Fekula, 1999). This latter effort involves both curricular and co-curricular elements, identifying "five critical ingredients in effective college-based character education [to be] teaching about character; displaying character; demanding character; apprenticeship or practicing character; and reflecting on character" (p. 19).

Assessing Character

With campus character initiatives and programs competing with other interests in an environment of scarce and limited resources, questions concerning their influence and effect abound. Indeed, this has been a long-standing concern among educators considering the broad purposes of higher education (see Lingley, 1931). What are the outcomes of these interventions? Do they make a difference in the virtuous qualities of students who participate in them? Is an improved reasoning capacity evidenced in the choices students make in resolving various life issues and dilemmas? Answers to such questions depend on the availability of adequate assessment and measurement tools for documenting relevant gains.

A variety of approaches to assessing the dimensions of character development, quantitative as well as qualitative, cross-sectional and longitudinal, are found in the literature. They range from familiar survey formats to creative online portfolio assessments. They include measure of character antecedents and correlates (for example, prior service involvement and attitudes) and even specific value spectra assessed in various value surveys, such as the Schwartz Value Survey (SVI; Schwartz, 1992); the Rokeach Value Survey (Rokeach, 1973); and the Allport, Vernon, and Lindsey Study of Values (1970). They focus on character gains of individual students and also address the components and features of institutions and programs designed to influence and cultivate these outcomes.

Perhaps most common among measurement efforts have been various applications of inventories and surveys to assess dimensions of character and the institutional components that contribute to them. For example, Astin and Antonio (2000) used select items relative to "civic responsibility, cultural awareness and sensitivity, volunteerism, importance of raising a family, religious beliefs and convictions, and understanding of others" (p. 4) from Higher Education Research Institute (HERI) national survey data to evaluate the impact of types of student involvement and various institutional characteristics on character. They found the range of college experiences associated with character development to include "exposure to interdisciplinary courses, ethnic studies, and women's studies; participation in religious services and activities; social activities with students from a variety of racial and ethnic backgrounds; and participation in leadership education or training" (p. 6). Similarly, Kuh (1998) used existing data from the College Student Experiences Questionnaire (CSEQ) to assess the effects of "values-centered institutions," concluding that creating a college of character entails a mission-articulated emphasis on character development, a holistic talent development philosophy, faculty and staff committed to the personal development of students, careful monitoring of policies and practices for consistency and commitment to character development, assessment of students' experiences, and cultivation of a character-building culture. A third example of this approach comes in the form of the DePaul Values Project (Filkins and Ferrari, 2003), wherein students report through an annual survey their perceptions of the institution's core mission and values, information that is helpful in connecting students' attitudes and behaviors to character-building opportunities and experiences.

Other forms of assessment have focused on examining the developmental progression of students' meaning-making structures relative to principled thinking (Rest, 1979) and moral maturity (the Moral Judgment Interview, or MJI; Colby and others, 1979). Numerous studies have employed the Defining Issues Test (DIT; King and Mayhew, 2002) and the MJI, for example, to evaluate students' level of moral reasoning and the nature of their reasons given for various moral judgments.

Some recent efforts to address measurement in this domain have included the use of self-assessment rubrics and protocols, development of real and virtual portfolios, and online assessment techniques. For example, from the U.S. Air Force Academy program noted earlier a self-assessment, paper-and-pencil Character Assessment Rating Scale is used to solicit student reports of the frequency of their own behaviors regarding twelve dimensions of the concept of character: integrity, honesty, loyalty, selflessness, compassion, competency, respectfulness, fairness, responsibility and self-discipline, decisiveness, spiritual appreciation, and cooperativeness. Others have argued that quantitative measures risk oversimplifying what is essentially an integrated constellation of personal attributes (Kuh, 1998), suggesting that qualitative assessments (student journals, papers, performance) might better lend themselves to a richer documentation of relevant outcomes (Colby, Ehrlich, Beaumont, and Stephens, 2003; Ramaley, 2000). Alverno College has long been a leader in the use of such techniques, pioneering creation and analysis of portfolios of student work and performance observations judged on the basis of public, developmental criteria (Alverno College Faculty, 1994). Similarly, at the University of California-Berkeley, an Evaluation System for Experiential Education (ESEE; http://gse.berkeley.edu/research/slc/evaluation.html) uses focus groups, in addition to many of the same techniques mentioned earlier, to assess the outcomes of service-learning courses, incorporating information about faculty goals and outcomes, and community agency perceptions as well.

A final illustration of a recent and innovative integration of character assessment and technology is found in the Virtual Professional Portfolio Plan at St. Michael's College, where students have the opportunity to submit online documentation relative to their "ability . . . to judge what is right, care deeply about and desire what is right, and do what is right—even in the presence of pressures from the outside and temptations on the inside" (http://www2.smcvt.edu/src/career/VPPP).

In summary, these various assessment approaches are important not only for evaluating the efficacy of campus character development interventions and programs, but also for communicating institutional goals, expectations, and practices in regard to character outcomes. Documenting these dimensions can offer critical formative feedback for supporting institutional efforts in this direction and for improving overall outcomes.

Conclusion

Rather than exact, the language and understandings of character development during the college years embrace a range of concepts and practices. It is not surprising, then, that its aims are at times unclear and its relevance to the educational mission held in question by some. Nevertheless, renewed interest in this domain has heightened the sensitivity of educators to consider once again that the relationships between learning and living and the goals associated with character development are perhaps inevitable. Finally, in an increasingly competitive enrollment environment, institutions willing to examine how they measure up and act on such concerns might be those who will ultimately prove most successful in responding to a public that expects at least as much.

References

Allport, G. W., Vernon, P., and Lindsey, G. *Manual for the Study of Values* (3rd ed.). Boston: Houghton Mifflin, 1970.

Alverno College Faculty. *Student Assessment-as-Learning at Alverno College.* Milwaukee, Wis.: Alverno College Institute, 1994.

Astin, H. S., and Antonio, A. L. "Building Character in College." *About Campus,* 2000, 5(5), 3–7.

Barlow, C. B., Jordan, M., and Hendrix, W. H. "Character Assessment: An Examination of Leadership Levels." *Journal of Business and Psychology,* 2003, 17(4), 563–584.

Berkowitz, M. W. "A Primer for Evaluating a Character Education Initiative." (n.d.) Retrieved July 7, 2004, from http://www.character.org/resources/ceppublications/index.cgi?file=primer#primer.

Berkowitz, M. W., and Fekula, M. J. "Educating for Character." *About Campus,* 1999, 4(5), 17–22.

Blimling, G. "Developing Character in College Students." *NASPA Journal,* 1990, 27(4), 266–274.

Bloland, H. G. "Postmodernism and Higher Education." *Journal of Higher Education,* 1995, 66(5), 521–559.

Boyer, E. L. *College: The Undergraduate Experience in America.* New York: HarperCollins, 1987.

Brubacher, J. S., and Rudy, W. *Higher Education in Transition* (3rd ed.). New York: HarperCollins, 1976.

Colby, A., Ehrlich, T., Beaumont, E., and Stephens, J. *Educating Citizens.* San Francisco: Jossey-Bass, 2003.

Colby, A., and others. *Standard Form Scoring Manual* (Parts 1–4). Cambridge, Mass.: Center for Moral Education, Harvard University, 1979.

Crookston, B. "A Design for an Intentional Democratic Community." In D. A. DeCoster and P. Mable (eds.), *Student Development and Education in College Residence Halls.* Washington, D.C.: American College Personnel Association, 1974.

DeMarco, D. *The Heart of Virtue.* San Francisco: Ignatius Press, 1996.

Eddy, E. D., Jr. *Colleges for Our Land and Time: The Land-Grant Idea in American Education.* New York: HarperCollins, 1957.

Evaluation System for Experiential Education (ESEE). University of California, Berkeley, n.d. Retrieved July 7, 2004, from http://gse.berkeley.edu/research/slc/evaluation.html

Filkins, J. W., and Ferrari, J. R. "The DePaul Values Project and the DeVI: Assessing Students' Perceptions of a Private University's Core Mission and Values." *Journal of College and Character,* 2003, 2, 1–39. Retrieved July 7, 2004, from http://www.collegevalues.org/articles.cfm.

Gilligan, C. *In a Different Voice: Psychological Theory and Women's Development.* Cambridge, Mass.: Harvard University Press, 1982.

Hacker, A. "The Decline of Higher Learning." *New York Review of Books,* Feb. 13, 1986.

Isaacs, D. *Character Building: A Guide for Parents and Teachers.* Dublin, Ireland: Four Courts Press, 1976.

Kellogg Commission on the Future of State and Land-Grant Universities. *Renewing the Covenant: Learning, Discovery, and Engagement in a New Age and a Different World.* Washington, D.C.: National Association of State Universities and Land-Grant Colleges, 2000.

Kellogg Commission on the Future of State and Land-Grant Universities. *Returning to Our Roots: Executive Summaries.* Washington, D.C.: National Association of State Universities and Land-Grant Colleges, 2001.

King, P., and Mayhew, M. "Moral Judgment Development in Higher Education: Insights from the Defining Issues Test." *Journal of Moral Education,* 2002, *31*(3), 247–270.

Kohlberg, L. "Stage and Sequence: The Cognitive Developmental Approach to Socialization." In D. A. Goslin (ed.), *Handbook of Socialization Theory and Research.* Chicago: Rand-McNally, 1969.

Kuh, G. D. "Shaping Student Character." *Liberal Education,* 1998, *84*(3), 1823.

Lickona, T. "Character Education: Seven Crucial Issues." *Action in Teacher Education,* 1998, *20*(4), 77–84.

Lingley, C. R. "Does College Develop Character?" *Journal of Higher Education,* 1931, *2*(4), 177–182.

Lopez, S., and Snyder, C. *Positive Psychological Assessment: A Handbook of Models and Measures.* Washington, D.C.: American Psychological Association, 2003.

Pawelski, J. O. "The Promise of Positive Psychology for the Assessment of Character." *Journal of College and Character,* 2003, *2*, 1–6. Retrieved July 7, 2004, from http://www.collegevalues.org/articles.cfm?a=1&id=1141.

Peterson, C., and Seligman, M. *Values in Action (VIA) Classification of Strengths Manual.* 2003. Retrieved July 7, 2004, from http://www.positivepsychology.org/taxonomy.htm.

Ramaley, J. "Embracing Civic Responsibility." *AAHE Bulletin,* 2000, *52*(7), 9–13, 20.

Rest, J. R. *Development in Judging Moral Issues.* Minneapolis: University of Minnesota Press, 1979.

Rokeach, M. *The Nature of Human Values.* San Francisco: Jossey-Bass, 1973.

Schwartz, S. H. "Universals in the Content and Structure of Values: Theoretical Advances and Empirical Tests in 20 Countries." In M. Zanna (ed.), *Advances in Experimental Social Psychology* (vol. 25, pp. 1–65). Orlando, Fla.: Academic Press, 1992.

Seligman, M. "The President's Address." In *American Psychological Association 1998 Annual Report,* 1998. Retrieved July 7, 2004, from http://www.positivepsychology.org/aparep98.htm.

Smith, H. *Why Religion Matters: The Fate of the Human Spirit in an Age of Disbelief.* New York: HarperCollins, 2001.

Whiteley, J. *Character Development in College Students* (vol. 1). Schenectady, N.Y.: Character Research Press, 1982.

Wingspread Group on Higher Education. *An American Imperative: Higher Expectations for Higher Education.* Racine, Wis.: Johnson Foundation, 1993.

C. CARNEY STRANGE *is professor of higher education and student affairs at Bowling Green State University in Ohio.*

The authors examine the college conditions that contribute to character development, using data from the National Survey of Student Engagement (NSSE).

College and Character: Insights from the National Survey of Student Engagement

George D. Kuh, Paul D. Umbach

Character is variously defined. At one level of abstraction, most would agree that character is a window into personality, a constellation of attitudes, values, ethical considerations, and behavioral patterns that represent what people believe and value, how they think, and what they do. When we say someone has "character," we mean that one exhibits admirable traits in both intellectual and behavioral dimensions of public and private life and acts with integrity in that behavior is congruent with values and beliefs. People of "good" character, then, work toward the public good, with integrity and personal responsibility that reflect their examined understanding of their ethical responsibility to self and the larger community.

Developing character was a primary goal of undergraduate education in the colonial colleges (Rudolph, 1990). The collegiate experience was intended to shape students' attitudes and values as much as to stretch their intellect and expand their knowledge of the world. Indeed, the initial wave of American colleges was founded by denominational groups in no small part to preserve an important facet of character: their religious heritage, beliefs, and values. As higher education expanded to accommodate a growing number of participants, the new institutions that emerged introduced other priorities. Existing colleges became more secular in their mission, philosophy, and curricular orientation. Thus the emphasis that colleges placed on character development declined commensurately, except at those institutions that retained more than a titular connection with their sponsoring denomination (Horowitz, 1987).

Even as American higher education became more secular in orientation and practice, most institutions continued to include among their educational purposes one or more that underscored the importance of providing students with the opportunity to discover, refine, and test their character. Within the past decade, there has been a resurgence of interest in intentionally promoting civic engagement during college, stemming from several factors. Among the most pronounced are the national scandals and public embarrassments that began with Watergate and continued through Enron, the Catholic Church, and wrongdoings by Olympic athletes and organizers. These enduring, prickly events have left an ugly mark on the American psyche and are unpleasant reminders of what can happen when the bedrock of individual and corporate values and ethical systems are left unattended and atrophy.

Though some argue that the values and ethical systems of individual students are pretty well set before they come to college, the literature suggests that the college experience can at the least accentuate a student's values development trajectory (Astin, 1993; Feldman and Newcomb, 1969; Pascarella and Terenzini, 1991). That is, college can further support and channel maturational processes under way to crystallize and integrate the attitudinal and values dimension of a student's identity (Chickering and Reisser, 1993). In a small fraction of cases, perhaps no more than 10 percent (Clark and others, 1972), college may have a transforming effect, resulting in substantial reorganization of one's personality. The impact of college on values development is mediated significantly by peer interaction (Astin, 1977; Astin, Sax, and Avalos, 1999; Kuh, 1993, 1995; Pascarella and Terenzini, 1991). Moreover, college is likely to have a shaping influence on values development of students who are actively involved in both academic and out-of-class activities. Thus it stands to reason that character development is enhanced by taking part in a variety of educationally purposeful activities.

If college attendance is to affect, even marginally, the character of its students, what conditions must be present? Which college experiences contribute to character development? Most of the theorizing and empirical studies about character development during the college years, as we have defined it, are small *n* or single-institution studies (for example, Baxter Magolda, 2001; Heath, 1968; Parks, 2000). Aside from a few classic multiple institution studies (see Astin, 1977, 1993; Jacob, 1957; Sanford, 1962), there is little information to estimate the extent to which the undergraduate experience has a positive, shaping influence on the character of contemporary college students across a large number of institutions. Moreover, most of the studies addressing character building during the undergraduate years focus on character-related attitudes and values; few studies emphasize the behavior that shapes or is associated with character development. Yet how students behave—what they do during college—is essential for knowing whether institutions are providing the type of experience inside and outside the classroom that has a positive shaping influence on character. In addition, such evidence is arguably a precursor of what one might expect of college graduates in later life.

Purpose and Overview

This chapter offers some insight into the activities and collegiate experiences that are associated with character development. Our data come from the National Survey of Student Engagement (NSSE), an annual survey of college students that focuses on the amount of time and energy students devote to educationally purposeful activities. The NSSE national database allows us to answer two questions relevant to character development: (1) What experiences during college are related to student self-reports of their character development? (2) Do some institutions and institutional types differentially affect character development? That is, do students at some types of institution, such as denominational colleges, report greater gains in the areas that contribute to character development?

First, we describe the nature of the information and analytical approaches we employed to answer these two questions. We then summarize major findings from the analysis. We close with implications and ideas for additional research that might yield insight into character development as part of the undergraduate experience.

Insights from NSSE about Character Development During College

The National Survey of Student Engagement is an annual survey of first-year and senior students that measures the degree to which students participate in educational practices that prior research shows are linked to valued outcomes of college (Chickering and Gamson, 1987; Kuh, 2001). For all practical purposes, the participating institutions are representative of the four-year college population by Carnegie type, sector, and region of the county, and in other dimensions.

The NSSE survey instrument, *The College Student Report*, asks students about their experiences in four areas: (1) the amount of time and effort devoted to various in-class and out-of-class activities, including reading and writing, and the frequency with which students participate in class discussions, make class presentations, work with peers on problem solving, and interact with faculty members; (2) participation in enriching educational activities (study abroad, internships, and so on); (3) gains in personal and educational development; and (4) perceptions of the college environment, including overall satisfaction with college and quality of academic advising. As Sweet Briar College president Elisabeth Muhlenfeld said, the NSSE items represent "an effort to get at the habits of mind."

The survey relies on student self-reports. A fair amount of research (Baird, 1976; Berdie, 1971; Pace, 1985; Pike, 1995; Pohlmann, 1974) has shown that self-reports are likely to be valid if (1) the information requested is known to the respondents; (2) the questions are phrased clearly and unambiguously; (3) the questions refer to recent activities; (4) the respondents think the questions merit a serious and thoughtful response; and (5) answering the questions does not threaten, embarrass, or violate the privacy of the respondent or encourage the respondent to respond in socially desirable ways (Kuh and Hu, 2001). The NSSE survey was designed to satisfy all of these conditions. Self-reported information is particularly relevant for measuring aspects of the college experience, such as character development, that cannot be easily assessed through other means. Moreover, the absence of widely used psychometrically sound measures of character development makes it difficult to assess the construct without incorporating student self-reports.

The sample used in this study is composed of 49,692 seniors who completed the NSSE survey in 2002 and 2003 from 568 four-year colleges and universities. Only seniors who started college at the institution from which they were about to graduate were included in the analysis because they had the most exposure to that institution. Other research shows that transfer students differ systematically in their engagement from their counterparts who start and persist to graduation at the same college or university (Kuh, 2003; National Survey of Student Engagement, 2002). For this reason, we excluded students who had transferred; this simplifies interpretation of findings and allows us to be more confident about our conclusions concerning differences by institutional type.

Data Analysis

The independent variables were various measures of student engagement and perceptions of the campus. Student engagement was represented by three scales: (1) academic challenge, (2) active and collaborative learning, and (3) student-faculty interaction. The campus environment measure was made up of two subscales—interpersonal support and support for learning—as well as an overall satisfaction-with-college scale. We also used scales made up of subsets of items to reflect diversity-related activities and integrative learning experiences. Other studies (Antonio, 2001; Chang, 1999; Gurin, 1999; Milem and Hakuta, 2000; Umbach and Kuh, 2003) show that experiences with diversity have a positive effect on a variety of outcomes. Integration is a form of deep learning that requires acquisition of knowledge, skills, and competencies across a variety of academic and social activities into a meaningful whole. Items contributing to the integration scale include such activities as incorporating ideas from various sources into a paper, making use of diverse perspectives in class discussions or writing projects, and putting together ideas and concepts from different courses

(National Survey of Student Engagement, 2003; Pike and Kuh, forthcoming; Pike, Kuh, and Gonyea, 2003).

To represent the dependent variable, character development, we selected twelve items from the self-reported gains section on the NSSE survey that reflect four related dimensions of character development. The question posed to students is, "To what extent has your experience at this institution contributed to your knowledge, skills and personal development in the following areas?" These are the four dimensions of character development and their contributing items:

1. Knowledge of self (three items):
   Understanding self
   Understanding people of other racial and ethnic backgrounds
   Working effectively with others
2. Ethical development and problem solving (two items):
   Developing a personal code of ethics
   Solving complex real-world problems
3. Civic responsibility (two items):
   Voting in local, state, and national elections
   Contributing to the welfare of one's community
4. General knowledge (five items):
   Acquiring a broad, general education
   Learning effectively on one's own
   Writing clearly and effectively
   Speaking clearly and effectively
   Thinking critically and analytically

Responses are scored on a four-point scale representing the amount of progress or gains for a student during college in each respective area, ranging from "very little" to "very much."

The data were analyzed in three stages. First, we used descriptive statistics to construct a profile of the dimensions of character development as they are represented on the NSSE survey. Second, because of the nested nature of the data and the intent to estimate institutional effects (Raudenbush and Bryk, 2002), we used hierarchical linear modeling (HLM) to explore student and institutional characteristics. Table 4.1 presents the descriptive statistics for the independent variables that relate to self-reported gains in character development. Because students at level one are nested within colleges at level two, HLM allows us to partition the variance between what can be attributed to colleges and what can be attributed to students.

At the student level, we include gender, age, race, student major, participation in Greek-letter organizations, grades, and full-time enrollment in our models. At the institutional level, we created dummy coded variables for the five Carnegie types: doctoral/research-extensive, doctoral/research-intensive, master's I and II, baccalaureate liberal arts, and baccalaureate

Table 4.1. Descriptive Statistics of Independent Variables Included in Models

	Mean	Std. Dev.	Min.	Max.
Independent Variables, Level 1				
Gender	0.65	0.48	0.00	1.00
Age	0.00	1.00	−1.48	12.93
African American	0.06	0.23	0	1
Native American	0.00	0.06	0	1
Asian Pacific American	0.05	0.22	0	1
Latino	0.03	0.18	0	1
Other minority	0.01	0.07	0	1
Major-humanities	0.15	0.36	0	1
Major-math and science	0.21	0.41	0	1
Major-professional	0.29	0.45	0	1
Major-social sciences (omitted category)	0.17	0.38	0	1
Major-other	0.19	0.39	0	1
Greek	0.17	0.38	0	1
Grades	0.00	1.00	−2.79	1.31
Full-time	0.90	0.30	0	1
Independent Variables, Level 2				
Doctoral/Research-Extensive	0.12	0.32	0	1
Doctoral/Research-Intensive	0.09	0.28	0	1
Master's I and II	0.42	0.49	0	1
Baccalaureate-liberal arts	0.18	0.38	0	1
Baccalaureate-general	0.14	0.35	0	1
Urban	0.53	0.50	0	1
Suburban	0.24	0.42	0	1
Town/rural	0.23	0.42	0	1
Private	0.57	0.49	0	1
Undergraduate head count	0	1	−0.86	4.93
Selectivity (Barron's, 2002)	0	1	−2.1	2.55
Religiously affiliated	0.35	0.48	0	1

general (McCormick, 2001). To determine whether character development of students varied with type of institution, baccalaureate liberal arts colleges were designated as the omitted group because as a set of schools they had the highest overall mean score on the aggregated character development measures (Figure 4.1). In addition, a sizeable percentage of baccalaureate liberal arts colleges still have strong ties with their founding denomination and claim to place a significant emphasis on character-related matters both in the curriculum and in out-of-class activities, such as offering daily chapel and community service. Therefore we included a religious affiliation variable at level two. Additionally, we examined sector (public, private), urbanicity (urban, suburban, small town or rural), size (total undergraduate headcount), and a measure of selectivity (derived from the 2002 *Barron's College Guide*).

It is common to build hierarchical linear models in stages. In the first stage of model building, we create the within (or the student-level) model

Figure 4.1. Self-Reported Gains in Character Development Score Among NSSE 2002–03 Seniors

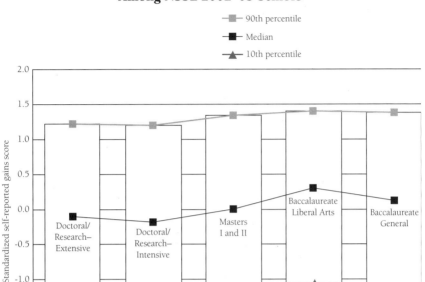

allowing the intercept to vary, thereby partitioning the variance that can be attributed to the institution. In the second stage, we build our full model by including level two predictors in our model. Because many of our level two predictors are highly correlated, we included each measure individually in our level two models.

In the third and final stage of the analysis, we built a series of hierarchical linear models to explore the relationships between character development and student engagement in educationally purposeful activities. We also examine the impact of perception of the campus environment and satisfaction on character development.

Because the number of students used in these analyses is large, it is important not only to examine statistical significance but also to understand the magnitude of difference. To understand substantive differences between students' character development scores for baccalaureate liberal arts colleges and other types of institutions, we calculated effect sizes (Rosenthal and Rosnow, 1991). The effect size is the proportion of a standard deviation change in the dependent variable as a result of a one-unit change in a dependent variable. We standardized all of the continuous independent and dependent measures in the models, so the unstandardized coefficients represent effect sizes. The larger the effect size, the more likely the difference between groups or institutional types reflects performance that warrants serious discussion and perhaps intervention. Following the suggestion of Rosenthal and Rosnow (1991), we considered an effect size of .10 or less to reflect a trivial difference, between .10 and .30 to be small, between .30 and .50 moderate, and greater than .50 large.

How Does Student Engagement Shape Character?

Our descriptive analyses show that students at baccalaureate liberal arts colleges report greater gains in character development than students at other types of colleges (Figure 4.1). Students at doctoral institutions report the lowest gains in character development during college.

Among the activities likely to contribute to character development are doing community service or working on a project in the community that is related to a course, volunteerism, the frequency with which students are exposed to diversity in the classroom, talking with students from other races and ethnicities, or having conversations with students who have different political and social views. Among the students who are more likely to experience diversity (and who may well report greater gains in character development) are students of color (contrasted with white students), traditional-aged students (contrasted with older students), women, and first-year students.

More than 60 percent participated in a community project during college (Figure 4.2), and most seniors (90+ percent) report encountering diverse perspectives in their classes. These experiences likely challenge students to develop novel or new ways of thinking and approaching issues, consistent with the challenge-and-support principle introduced by Nevitt Sanford (1962) and subsequently elaborated by others. Even so, about 15 percent of all seniors seem to get through the last year of college without having a serious conversation with a fellow student from another race and ethnicity. In part, this may be because of the self-segregation that occurs once a student leaves a campus residence hall and moves off campus. At the same time, the vast majority of students—about 82 percent—indicate that their college experience contributed substantially ("very much" or "quite a bit") to their ability to work effectively with others (Figure 4.3). Similarly, about 60 percent think college contributed substantially to their developing a systematic code of ethics. Especially troubling and disappointing is that more than half of all seniors say that their college experience had very little or an insignificant effect on the likelihood that they would vote in a local or national election (Figure 4.3).

Institutional "Averages" Don't Tell the Whole Character Development Story

One consistent, mildly provocative finding from the NSSE project is that the variance within an institution on any given measure is often greater than the variance between institutions including types of institutions. Figure 4.4

Figure 4.2. All NSSE 2002–03 Seniors Responding Having Never Participated

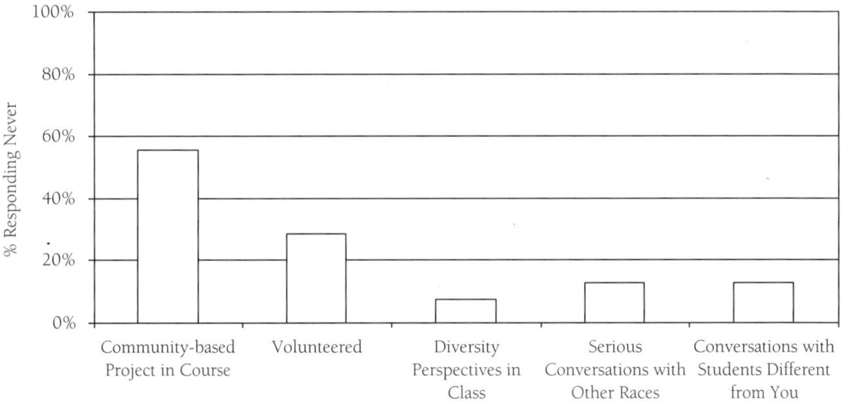

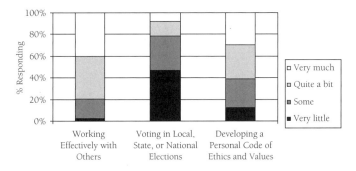

Figure 4.3. NSSE 2002–03 Senior Reports of Contribution of College Experience

shows the average character development score (based on the arithmetic sum of responses to the items contributing to the four dimensions of character development described earlier) for five Carnegie types. As mentioned earlier, students at baccalaureate liberal arts colleges report making greater gains in character development, followed by their peers at baccalaureate general colleges; master's-granting institutions; and the two largest institutions, the doctoral/research university-extensive and doctoral/research university-intensive. The difference in the median scores between these institution types is not great, but the variation in character development gains within the respective types of institution is quite substantial, stretching more than two standard deviations for the middle 80 percent of scores on these measures. That is, although the average character development score is higher at a baccalaureate liberal arts college, nonetheless a substantial number of students score well below their average peers at doctoral/research university-extensives. Thus character development is not

Figure 4.4. Highest (left band) and Lowest (right band) Scoring NSSE 2002–03 Institutions on Self-Reported Character Development Gains

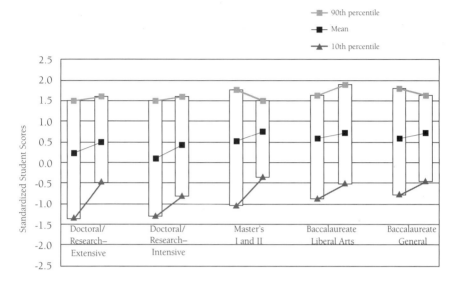

exclusively a function of small, residential, denominationally sponsored colleges.

Figure 4.4 shows this in starker relief, presenting the highest-scoring and lowest-scoring institutions from each category. The baccalaureate liberal arts college selected to represent the middle of its distribution has a relatively high average score, but a sizeable fraction of its students score much lower on the character development measure than the typical students at some other master's-granting institutions and even some large doctoral/research-extensive universities. The highest-scoring master's institution has a relatively compressed range in terms of character development relative to many other institutions. Something significant may well be happening at this institution to produce such a pattern of findings.

Interestingly, those institutions that tend to score highest on character development attract students that are fairly homogeneous in terms of their background characteristics. They tend to be liberal arts colleges and a healthy proportion of general baccalaureate colleges. At the same time, students at these institutions tend to have more diversity-related experiences, even though these institutions generally have less structural diversity than larger public universities that enroll a larger number of ethnic minority students. Indeed, most of these institutions have relatively low structural diversity. We examined this phenomenon more closely in another study (Umbach and Kuh, 2003) and discovered that structural diversity was not the explanation for higher frequency of diversity-related experiences. Rather, something was

Figure 4.5. Self-Reported Gains in Character Development Score Among NSSE 2002–03 Seniors

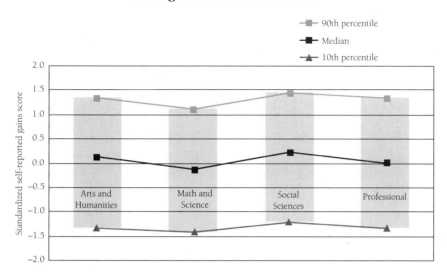

going on within these institutions that made it possible for students to inter-act more frequently with those (relatively few in number) members from other races and ethnicities who were present. It is also likely that the cur-riculum itself presented students with more opportunity to reflect on and deal with diverse perspectives.

As Figure 4.5 indicates, students in certain fields report a greater level of character development than others. Mildly surprising, perhaps, is that students in preprofessional fields such as health sciences and prelaw report gaining more in character development than their colleagues in the tradi-tional arts and sciences fields.

Multivariate Analysis

The findings from our descriptive analyses suggest some important institu-tional and student differences in gains in character development. We explore this further in our multivariate analyses. Table 4.2 displays the student-level coefficients predicting character development and the charac-ter development subscales. Students of color report significantly greater gains than white students in character development. On every measure, African Americans, Native Americans, and Latinos indicate greater gains than whites. For three of the five measures, Asian Pacific Americans score higher than whites.

As suggested by our descriptive statistics, the level of gain in character development reported by students varies by major. Students in the social sciences report the highest gains in general character development, civic

Table 4.2. Statistically Significant* Student-Level Coefficients (Represented in Effect Sizes)

	Character Development	Knowledge of Self and Others	Ethical Development and Problem Solving	Civic Responsibility	General Knowledge
Gender		0.09		0.06	0.08
Age	0.01	0.00		0.02	0.03
African American	0.18	0.13	0.09	0.25	0.19
Native American	0.28	0.21	0.20	0.26	0.26
Asian Pacific American	0.02	0.14	0.07		−0.07
Latino	0.21	0.19	0.17	0.17	0.19
Other minority					
Major-humanities	−0.09		−0.13	−0.17	−0.02
Major-math and science	−0.20	−0.16	−0.08	−0.33	−0.16
Major-professional	−0.09	0.02	−0.03	−0.18	−0.11
Major-other	−0.12	−0.02	−0.05	−0.21	−0.12
Greek	0.12	0.08	0.10	0.15	0.08
Grades	0.11	0.07	0.07	0.05	0.12
Full-time	0.15	0.15	0.14	0.11	0.11

*All coefficients presented are statistically significant, $p < .01$.

responsibility, and general knowledge. Math and science majors report the lowest gains on nearly every character development measure.

Table 4.3 presents the institution-level coefficients predicting gains in character development. In general, students at liberal arts colleges report greater gains in character development than students from other institution types. However, students at baccalaureate-general institutions report gains in knowledge of self and others, ethical development and problem solving, and civic responsibility that are not statistically significantly different from students at liberal arts colleges.

Although the effect sizes are somewhat modest, it seems that students at private colleges indicate greater gains in character development than students at public colleges. Additionally, institutional size is negatively related to reported gains in character development. As we expected, students at religiously affiliated institutions report greater gains in character development than students at unaffiliated institutions.

Table 4.4 displays the results from a fully controlled model (all institutional and individual controls) where each engagement, campus climate, and integrative measure is added to the model. Our findings suggest that engagement in effective educational practices generally enhances students' self-reported change in character development. Additionally, students at campuses that create a supportive campus climate and offer integrative experiences are more likely to indicate growth in character development.

Table 4.3. Statistically Significant* Institution-Level Coefficients (Represented in Effect Sizes)

	Character Development	Knowledge of Self and Others	Ethical Development and Problem Solving	Civic Responsibility	General Knowledge
Carnegie					
Doctoral/ Research-Extensive	− 0.25		− 0.15	− 0.17	− 0.32
Doctoral/ Research-Intensive	− 0.30	− 0.14	− 0.18	− 0.20	− 0.35
Master's II and II	− 0.16	− 0.07	− 0.10		− 0.21
Baccalaureate general	− 0.09	− 0.03	− 0.02	0.01	− 0.17
Sector					
Private	0.14	0.07	0.13	0.09	0.14
Urbanicity					
Suburban					
Town/rural					
Selectivity					
Barron's		− 0.03			0.04
Size					
Undergrad head count	− 0.06		− 0.05	− 0.06	− 0.07
Religiously affiliated					
Affiliated	0.19	0.10	0.18	0.20	0.15

*All coefficients presented are statistically significant, $p < .01$.

Limitations

One limitation of this study is the measure of character development constructed from the NSSE survey. There are surely additional relevant dimensions of character that are not captured by these NSSE items. Another limitation is related to the validity of self-reported gains. As Pascarella (2001) and others point out, gain scores may be confounded by students' entering characteristics. Though Pike (1999) provides some evidence to suggest that gain scores are not significantly related to entering ability, it is likely that students who are committed to character development select a college that emphasizes character-promoting activities (such as community service).

Additionally, self-selection bias should be considered when interpreting the results. In the college choice process, students who seek to enhance their character may in fact be selecting particular colleges because they appear to foster an environment that would offer such opportunities. This possible self-selection may bias the relationship between religiously affiliated institutions and liberal arts colleges and the dependent measures of this study.

Table 4.4. Student-Level Coefficients (Represented in Effect Sizes)*
of Engagement, Climate, and Integrative Experiences from Fully
Controlled Model

	Character Development	Knowledge of Self and Others	Ethical Development and Problem Solving	Civic Responsibility	General Knowledge
Engagement					
Academic challenge	0.48	0.36	0.39	0.30	0.48
Active and collaborative	0.44	0.34	0.37	0.27	0.43
Student-faculty interaction	0.42	0.35	0.35	0.33	0.36
Volunteering	0.31	0.26	0.23	0.40	0.21
Learning community	0.32	0.30	0.28	0.35	0.22
Supportive Campus Climate					
Supportive campus	0.58	0.53	0.49	0.45	0.49
Interpersonal support	0.45	0.41	0.37	0.32	0.40
Support for learning	0.54	0.49	0.34	0.45	0.43
Satisfaction	0.53	0.46	0.42	0.30	0.48
Integrative Experiences					
Integration	0.48	0.39	0.40	0.34	0.45
Diversity-related activities	0.32	0.32	0.26	0.24	0.25

*All coefficients presented are statistically significant, $p < .01$.

Implications

As with many other aspects of undergraduate education, colleges reap what they sow. Thus the mission, curriculum, and student's experiences must be aligned with character development as an intended outcome. If character development is important, institutions should both expect and require students to do the things that develop character. This would include those experiences that are connected to a greater level of character development, such as doing community service as part of a regular course and experiencing diversity. To do this successfully, awareness is a key first step; that is, students must actually know about opportunities to test and reflect on their values and beliefs in a way that induces them to integrate what they are learning with who they are becoming. Thus messages must be sent to students long before they arrive as to the value of developing a coherent constellation of values, ethics, and behavioral patterns that prepare them to live a civically responsible, socially aware, and economically productive life after college. Students must also be told early on, and then institutions must consistently reinforce the message, that opportunities will be presented for students to experience and integrate what they are learning from their courses with their social, political, and cultural lives. Then institutions must intentionally organize the students' in-class and out-of-class experiences so that they are exposed to the kind of activities and events that push them further along the character development path.

Given the variety of educational purposeful activities that are associated with character development, no one program is likely to have the desired effect on character development. That is, character cannot be "taught" in a single course, or developed as part of an orientation program or capstone experience. Rather, the multiple dimensions of character are cultivated through a variety of experiences that take place over an extended period of time in the company of others who are undergoing similar experiences. To this end, institutions should intentionally create opportunities for students inside and outside the classroom to integrate their experiences in a manner that nurtures character development. Indeed, it takes a whole campus to develop a student's character.

It is not surprising that smaller, religiously affiliated colleges appear to create an environment that is character-enhancing. To no small degree, character development is a focal point of the mission and culture of many of these institutions. Yet of the ten highest-scoring institutions on our global measure of character development, only two are unabashedly denominational; both are Catholic colleges, and several others are only nominally affiliated with a denomination. Three of the institutions are historically black colleges (one of which is public), and two others are among the more experimental and reformist in terms of their educational philosophy and pedagogical approach. Surprisingly, perhaps, four are single-sex colleges. It's not clear, then, what these schools have in common except that they tend to be small (eight of the ten schools have approximately two thousand students or less) and on average they all engage their students in value-driven activities that promote application and integration of classroom material to real-world issues.

Though we cannot speak in definitive terms about all the strongest-performing colleges on our measure of character development, we know enough about several of these institutions to say with confidence that they go well beyond simply offering opportunities for their students to reflect, refine, and test their values, ethics, and attitudes. That is, a campus can create a set of activities that theoretically should contribute to character development, but unless students actually experience or take part in those activities one cannot anticipate the desired effect. Institutions where students report making progress in development of character present a range of character-testing activities and require their students to take part in more than a few.

To know whether a school is actually achieving its character development purposes, a systematic assessment program is needed, one that provides feedback to close the loop and to guide and document initiatives that are designed for this effect. Systematic, ongoing assessment can help identify those students who do not participate in such activities and learn why. In addition, adjustments can and should be made to various programs to be sure they are having the desired effect on character development. The

American Democracy Project of the American Association of State Colleges and Universities, sponsored by the *New York Times,* is one such effort to assess the impact of promoting civic engagement and student participation in allied activities inside and outside the classroom, with NSSE among other tools being used in the effort.

Conclusion

This study adds to our understanding of the college activities and institutional characteristics that are related to character development during the undergraduate years. As colleges and universities prepare students to conduct their lives in an ethically enlightened manner and in an increasingly diverse democracy, they would do well to stitch into their policies and practices activities that give students firsthand experience with issues that the larger society is grappling with through community involvement, service learning, and other assignments. Opportunities to interact across racial, religious, and socioeconomic lines also seem to be important to character development, as is a campus environment that emphasizes values-based curricular and co-curricular initiatives and induces student participation in these complementary activities.

References

Antonio, A. L. "Diversity and the Influence of Friendship Groups in College." *Review of Higher Education,* 2001, 25(1), 63–89.

Astin, A. W. *Four Critical Years.* San Francisco: Jossey-Bass, 1977.

Astin, A. W. *What Matters in College: Four Critical Years Revisited.* San Francisco: Jossey-Bass, 1993.

Astin, A. W., Sax, L. J., and Avalos, J. "Long-Term Effects of Volunteerism During the Undergraduate Years." *Review of Higher Education,* 1999, 22(2), 187–202.

Baird, L. L. "Biographical and Educational Correlates of Graduate and Professional School Admissions Test Scores." *Educational and Psychological Measurement,* 1976, 36(2), 415–420.

Barron's Educational Series. *Profiles of American Colleges* (25th ed.). Hauppage, N.Y.: Barron's, 2002.

Baxter Magolda, M. B. *Making Their Own Way: Narratives for Transforming Higher Education to Promote Self-Development.* Sterling, Va.: Stylus, 2001.

Berdie, R. F. "Self-Claimed and Tested Knowledge." *Educational and Psychological Measurement,* 1971, 31(3), 629–636.

Chang, M. J. "Does Racial Diversity Matter? The Educational Impact of a Racially Diverse Undergraduate Population." *Journal of College Student Development,* 1999, 40, 377–395.

Chickering, A. W., and Gamson, Z. F. "Seven Principles for Good Practice in Undergraduate Education." *AAHE Bulletin,* 1987, 39(7), 3–7.

Chickering, A. W., and Reisser, L. *Education and Identity* (2nd ed.). San Francisco: Jossey-Bass, 1993.

Clark, B., and others. *Students and Colleges: Interaction and Change.* Berkeley: Center for Research and Development in Higher Education, University of California, 1972.

Feldman, K. A., and Newcomb, T. M. *The Impact of College on Students.* San Francisco: Jossey-Bass, 1969.

Gurin, P. "Expert Report of Patricia Gurin." In University of Michigan (ed.), The Compelling Need for Diversity in Higher Education, *Gratz et al.* v. *Bollinger et al*, no. 97–75231 (E.D. Mich.) and *Grutter et al.* v. *Bollinger et al.* no. 97–75928 (E.D. Mich.). Ann Arbor: University of Michigan, 1999.

Heath, D. H. *Growing up in College: Liberal Education and Maturity.* San Francisco: Jossey-Bass, 1968.

Horowitz, H. L. *Campus Life: Undergraduate Cultures from the End of the Eighteenth Century to the Present.* Chicago: University of Chicago Press, 1987.

Jacob, P. *Changing Values in College: An Exploratory Study of the Impact of College Teaching.* New York: HarperCollins, 1957.

Kuh, G. D. "Appraising the Character of College." *Journal of Counseling and Development,* 1993, *71*(6), 661–668.

Kuh, G. D. "The Other Curriculum: Out-of-Class Experiences Associated with Student Learning and Personal Development." *Journal of Higher Education,* 1995, *66*(2), 123–155.

Kuh, G. D. "Assessing What Really Matters to Student Learning: Inside the National Survey of Student Engagement." *Change,* 2001, *33*(3), 10–17, 66.

Kuh, G. D. "What We're Learning About Student Engagement from NSSE." *Change,* 2003, *35*(2), 24–32.

Kuh, G. D., and Hu, S. "The Effects of Student-Faculty Interaction in the 1990s." *Review of Higher Education,* 2001, *24,* 309–332.

McCormick, A. C. *The Carnegie Classification of Institutions of Higher Education, 2000 Edition.* Menlo Park, Calif.: Carnegie Foundation for the Advancement of Teaching, 2001.

Milem, J. F., and Hakuta, K. "The Benefits of Racial and Ethnic Diversity in Higher Education." In D. Wilds (ed.), *Minorities in Higher Education: Seventeenth Annual Status Report.* Washington, D.C.: American Council on Education, 2000.

National Survey of Student Engagement. *From Promise to Progress: How Colleges and Universities Are Using Student Engagement Results to Improve Collegiate Quality.* Bloomington: Center for Postsecondary Research, Indiana University, 2002.

National Survey of Student Engagement. *Converting Data into Action: Expanding the Boundaries of Institutional Improvement.* Bloomington: Center for Postsecondary Research, Indiana University, 2003.

Pace, C. R. *The Credibility of Student Self-Reports.* Los Angeles: Center for the Study of Evaluation, University of California, Los Angeles, 1985.

Parks, S. D. *Big Questions, Worthy Dreams: Mentoring Young Adults and the Search for Meaning, Faith, and Commitment.* San Francisco: Jossey-Bass, 2000.

Pascarella, E. T. "Using Student Self-Reported Gains to Estimate College Impact: A Cautionary Tale." *Journal of College Student Development,* 2001, *42*(5), 488–492.

Pascarella, E. T., and Terenzini, P. T. *How College Affects Students: Findings and Insights from Twenty Years of Research.* San Francisco: Jossey-Bass, 1991.

Pike, G. R. "Limitations of Using Students' Self-Reports of Academic Development as Proxies for Traditional Achievement Measures." Paper presented at the annual meeting of the Association for Institutional Research, Boston, 1995.

Pike, G. R. "The Constant Error of the Halo in Educational Outcomes Research." *Research in Higher Education,* 1999, *40*(1), 61–86.

Pike, G. R., and Kuh, G. D. "First- and Second-Generation College Students: A Comparison of Their Engagement and Intellectual Development." *Journal of Higher Education,* forthcoming.

Pike, G. R., Kuh, G. D., and Gonyea, R. M. "The Relationship Between Institutional Mission and Students' Involvement and Educational Outcomes." *Research in Higher Education,* 2003, *44,* 241–261.

Pohlmann, J. T. "A Description of Effective College Teaching in Five Disciplines as Measured by Student Ratings." *Research in Higher Education,* 1974, *4*(4), 335–346.

Raudenbush, S. W., and Bryk, A. A. *Hierarchical Linear Models* (2nd ed.). London: Sage, 2002.

Rosenthal, R., and Rosnow, R. L. *Essentials of Behavioral Research: Methods and Data Analysis* (2nd ed.). New York: McGraw-Hill, 1991.

Rudolph, F. *The American College and University: A History.* Athens: University of Georgia Press, 1990.

Sanford, N. "The Developmental Status of the Freshman." In N. Sanford (ed.), *The American College: A Psychological and Social Interpretation of the Higher Learning.* New York: Wiley, 1962.

Umbach, P., and Kuh, G. D. "Student Experiences with Diversity at Liberal Arts Colleges: Another Claim for Distinctiveness." Paper presented at the annual meeting of the Association for Institutional Research, Tampa, 2003.

GEORGE D. KUH is chancellor's professor of higher education and director of the Center for Postsecondary Research at Indiana University. His research interests include assessing student and institutional performance to improve the quality of the undergraduate experience.

PAUL D. UMBACH is assistant professor in the Department of Educational Policy and Leadership Studies, University of Iowa. His research examines the impact of organizations and social structures on student outcomes and the careers of faculty and senior administrators.

5

The authors assess the kinds of college experience that affect students' development of character.

The Impact of College on Character Development

Helen S. Astin, Anthony Lising Antonio

During the last two decades, colleges and universities have observed their students attach less and less importance to helping others and place more importance on gaining financial security. Furthermore, studies by Astin (1993), Boyer (1994), and Levine (1994) reveal growing individualism among college students and declining interest in politics and civic engagement. A number of higher education institutions have responded to these trends by establishing leadership development programs, volunteer and community service centers, and other programs designed to involve students as social participants in their institution and community. In addition to colleges and universities taking notice and acting to counter these trends, philanthropic organizations such as the John Templeton Foundation have also been engaged in developing and promoting civic values among youth. For example, for a number of years the Templeton Foundation has been publicly honoring colleges and universities that engage intentionally in developing character among college students. Despite those efforts, little research has been done to help us understand the role college actually plays in character development. What kinds of college experience in the curriculum and the

A version of this study appeared as an article, "Building Character in College," in *About Campus,* Nov.-Dec. 2000, 5(5), pp. 3–7 (©2000 American College Personnel Association and Jossey-Bass, used with permission of John Wiley & Sons, Inc.). The study was made possible by a grant from the John Templeton Foundation. We would like to express our appreciation to the foundation and to Arthur Schwartz in particular for support.

co-curriculum affect character development? Do particular institutional types provide a better context for character development?

The study reported in this chapter was designed to assess what kinds of college experience affect students' development of character. To accomplish this goal we decided to use information from a sample of colleges for which we had longitudinal data, collected from students at the start of the freshman year and four years later, so that we could identify specific college experiences that influence character development.

We were also interested in seeing whether institutions that claim to engage in intentional efforts to develop character in their students indeed succeed in those efforts. For this purpose, we identified a group of institutions that were honored by the Templeton Foundation as being exemplary in developing character, and we included their students in our study.

Data Source and Method of Analysis

Our database contained data on students attending 167 colleges and universities, of which 32 were selected by the John Templeton Foundation in their 1997–98 Honor Roll of Character Building Colleges. These longitudinal data were provided by the Higher Education Research Institute (HERI) at UCLA. A national sample of entering college freshmen were surveyed by HERI in the summer and fall of 1993 prior to college entry using the 1993 Student Information Form (SIF). The SIF is a four-page survey instrument that gathers an array of information, including students' high school activities; high school grades; and precollege attitudes, opinions, goals, and level of self-concept. The instrument is typically administered during college orientation and measures student characteristics prior to exposure to the college environment. A subset of these freshmen were surveyed again four years later by HERI using the 1997 College Student Survey (CSS). This follow-up survey contained measures of student behavior and involvement in college as well as measures of attitudes, goals, opinions, and self-concept that were identical in the SIF in order to assess change over four years of college. The final sample extracted for analysis included 9,792 students that responded to both the 1993 SIF and the 1997 CSS surveys.

In designing the analyses for this study, we first tried to define what we mean by *character*. We began with the notion that character represents values and behaviors reflected in how we interact with each other and in the moral choices we make every day. In conceptualizing the study, we were helped by Lasker and Moore's definition of moral development as "a progressive understanding of the process and principles through which social relationships and the order of society are created and maintained" (1980, p. 26).

Since one of the authors of the present study was familiar with the Templeton Foundation's Honor Roll selection procedures, we considered in our choice of outcome measures the criteria used in selecting the

Templeton-honored schools. In 1997, colleges were invited by the foundation to submit descriptions of programs and efforts designed specifically to help students develop the traits and values that translate into moral behavior and action. The colleges responded to a set of questions sent to them by the foundation, among them "In what ways does your college provide support for students who seek spiritual meaning in their lives?" "How does your college define, promote, and defend a set of core moral values that reinforce standards of behavior and student expectations?" "What service-learning opportunities are available to your students?" "What initiatives or projects has your college implemented to enable students to understand and appreciate the college as a moral community?" In judging the institutions with respect to efforts to build character, we assessed colleges on whether they had inspired students to develop and strengthen their moral reasoning skills, encouraged spiritual growth and moral values, made community-building experiences available, advocated a drug-free lifestyle, and conducted a critical assessment of character-building project activities.

Six measures (dependent variables) were chosen to complement and extend the literature on the moral and civic development of college students: civic and social values, cultural awareness, volunteerism, importance of family, religious beliefs and convictions, and understanding of others. Previous studies of moral and civic development have concentrated on measures of moral reasoning and civic values only (Pascarella and Terenzini, 1991). In this investigation, we examined the development of civic values, and in addition we studied values and self-assessments associated with community and cultural awareness, the family, and religious beliefs. Finally, we included a measure of volunteerism that encompasses actual student behavior (performing volunteer work in college) and a measure reflecting understanding of others.

Three of the dependent variables were composite measures whose constituent variables were derived through exploratory factor analyses: civic and social values, cultural awareness, and volunteerism. The measures that make up each composite variable (through a summation of the constituent variable scores) and the internal consistencies (alpha) for each composite are shown in the Appendix to this chapter. The importance of "raising a family" was asked as one in a list of student life goals, and "understanding of others" was asked as a self-assessed personal characteristic. "Religious beliefs and convictions" was a variable that assessed how students' religiosity changed and developed compared to the time of college entry. We admit that these measures are not by any means exhaustive operational definitions of moral character, but they do represent central elements in character as a "constellation of integrated moral, ethical, civic, humanitarian and spiritual values" (Kuh and Vesper, 1998, p. 1). They also reflect the goals of many programs designed to enhance character development reported by Templeton Honor Roll schools. For example, in describing how they met the criteria for selection, schools described spiritual growth being nurtured not only through religious practices such as attending chapel but also through service and volunteer work. Community-building experiences were acquired through service learning and community service or through development of multicultural learning communities. Schools also described using a formal series of leadership development activities to develop and strengthen students' "moral reasoning skills." These skills included the ability to make ethical choices and also understanding the views of people who differ from oneself, practicing an unbiased habit of mind, and treating others with fairness and civility.

To assess the impact of college on the development of character as reflected in these six outcome measures, we examined how students' college experiences and type of institution attended affect this development. It is well-known that college affects a student's cognitive development and has a major impact on personal and social development (Bowen, 1977). Character and values represent those aspects of students' personal development that are intricately intertwined with how they behave interpersonally and the moral choices they make daily. The college curriculum, the faculty, and the peer group can all influence character and values during the college years.

On the basis of the findings of studies reported by Pascarella and Terenzini in *How College Affects Students* (1991), the college experiences we attended to as important in character development included curricular and co-curricular experiences, faculty values and behaviors, and student peers' behaviors and attitudes. In designing the study and analysis, we were guided by a set of expectations:

- That developmental outcomes would vary with type of institution
- That faculty's values and behavior would have a direct effect on students' moral and character development
- That institutions modeling a culture of inclusion, respect of others, and a service orientation toward others would have a positive effect on students' development
- That the peer culture would have a strong effect on student outcomes
- That curricular and co-curricular experiences would affect students' character development

For our initial analyses we made two comparisons. First, we looked at how women and men differ on the character outcomes we chose to examine. We were interested in seeing whether women develop more of the character qualities as a result of their college experiences than do men. Given the special recognition of Templeton-honored schools for their attention to character development, we also compared Templeton to non-Templeton schools. In addition to these analyses, we used correlational analyses (hierarchical multiple regression) in order to examine how type of institution and specific college experiences affect character development, holding constant student characteristics at the time of college entry.

In drawing conclusions about the effects of institutions and their programs on building student character, one must recognize that students are not randomly assigned to institutions and programs, and this "self-selection" process must be considered in assessing the effect a college or university has on the development of moral character.

Results and Discussion

With respect to gender differences, we observed that after four years of college women exhibited a higher level of civic and social values, had done more volunteer work, and indicated a greater ability to understand others (see Table 5.1). Women also reported a significantly greater increase than did men in cultural awareness, their religious beliefs and convictions, and the importance they held for raising a family. In other words, four years after college entry the women in our sample exhibited significantly higher scores on all the measures of character development employed in this study. When we compared students who had attended Templeton-honored schools to students at other institutions, we found that students at Templeton schools had higher scores on four of the six measures of moral and character development: civic and social values, volunteerism, the importance of raising a family as a life goal, and religious beliefs and convictions (see Table 5.2). It is apparent, then, that both individual characteristics (gender) and the characteristics of the institution students attend (Templeton-honored schools versus not) contribute to character development. Employing correlational analyses enabled us to control for (hold constant) individual characteristics and thus isolate the specific type of institution and particular collegiate experiences that affect character development.

For these analyses, we examined a set of variables that describe the institutional environment and its culture. We expected that the type of institution (religious versus nonsectarian college, large versus small institution, university versus college) would affect students differently. We also anticipated that institutions promoting community service and volunteerism and those valuing diversity would be more likely to contribute to students' character development (for the composite measures representing these variables, see the Appendix to this chapter). We further believed that if students were immersed in a peer environment where they generally had strong civic values, valued the goal of raising a family, or had a strong religious orientation, such an environment would have an impact on their character development. Lastly, we analyzed measures of students' college involvement. The degree to which students became involved in college as well as the specific type of involvement activity in which they engage have been shown by Astin (1993) to be a primary contributor to development during the college years. In addition, a study of the development of civic values among college students by Pascarella, Ethington, and Smart (1988) further highlights the importance of involvement activities in civic development. In our study we chose

Table 5.1. Moral and Civic Development Outcomes: Differences by Gender

	Mean Score			
Outcome Variable	Women	Men	t(df)	2-tailed sig
Civic and social values	15.13	14.11	13.33(9532)	p < .001
Cultural awareness	15.57	15.43	3.15(9590)	p < .003
Volunteerism	5.84	5.22	14.54(9578)	p < .001
Goal: raise a family	3.18	3.13	3.16(9639)	p < .003
Religious beliefs and convictions	3.46	3.32	7.08(9645)	p < .001
Understanding of others	4.08	4.02	4.07(9682)	p < .001

Table 5.2. Moral and Civic Development Outcomes: Comparing Templeton Schools

	Mean Score			
Outcome Variable	Templeton	Non-Templeton	t(df)	2-tailed sig
Civic and social values	14.98	14.64	3.80(9576)	p < .001
Cultural awareness	15.52	15.51	0.18(9635)	p > .860
Volunteerism	5.82	5.52	5.89(9623)	p < .001
Goal: raise a family	3.22	3.15	3.29(9684)	p < .003
Religious beliefs and convictions	3.58	3.35	9.82(9690)	p < .001
Understanding of others	4.06	4.05	0.80(9727)	p > .420

to examine the effect of involvement in religious activities; leadership activities; volunteer work; and specific academic activities such as taking interdisciplinary, ethnic studies, and women's studies courses.

The results of our multivariate analyses demonstrated that selective institutions tended to have a negative impact, while religiously affiliated colleges generally have a positive effect on character development. Specifically, even when we hold constant entering student characteristics such as value orientation and social attitudes, Catholic colleges have a direct positive effect on students' civic and social values and goals for raising a family and an indirect effect on volunteerism and religious beliefs and convictions. Indirect effects are mediated through student experiences in curricular or co-curricular activities at those institutions. In other words, Catholic colleges appear to create opportunities or encourage students to engage in activities that benefit character development. Similarly, Protestant colleges appear to offer students activities that enhance gains in civic values, volunteerism, and religious beliefs and convictions. The selectivity of a college also had effects on three of the outcome measures, all of which were negative. More academically selective institutions appear to negatively affect the development of civic and social values, religious beliefs and convictions, and cultural awareness. Again, since involvement activities mediate these institutional effects, our results suggest that the campus culture of religious institutions fosters a setting in which character-enhancing activities are valued, while the culture of academically selective campuses may actually discourage such involvement.

What students do while in college and the kind of curricular and co-curricular experience they have is what makes the greatest difference in students' character development. The college experiences that were found to be critical and significant in the development of character included exposure to interdisciplinary courses, ethnic studies, and women's studies; participation in religious services and activities; socializing with students from a variety of racial and ethnic backgrounds; and participation in leadership education or training. Performing volunteer work while in college and having faculty who provide emotional support to students were also predictive of character development in students. The majority of these activities suggest that those broadening students' academic, social, and cultural perspectives are among the most important activities that contribute to students' character development.

A finding of particular interest in this study is that students who had done volunteer work *during the high school years* were precisely those who showed the most growth on all aspects of character. This finding suggests that volunteerism in high school may predispose students to partake in the opportunities and experiences in college that directly contribute to character development. This finding also suggests there is a cumulative and long-term effect of volunteerism. Colleges and universities interested in both maximizing the character development of individual students and creating a culture of volunteerism that enhances character development can begin addressing these goals by focusing on the importance of volunteerism in the precollegiate years as well as during college.

Leadership training programs and participation in student clubs also influenced character development as measured in this study. The findings concerning leadership training were not surprising given recent writings about the importance of leadership education for student development. Cress, Astin, Burkhardt, and Zimmerman-Oster (2001) have documented how leadership education positively affects self-awareness, clarification and development of values, and caring for social issues. Also, it is important to note that sociability across race contributes to students' sense of civic responsibility, cultural awareness, service to the community, religious beliefs, and understanding of others—all aspects of character. Research by Chang (1996) and Antonio (1998) has documented the importance of diversity in students' development while in college.

What about Templeton Honor Roll schools? Is there an independent institutional effect, beyond the nature of the students they tend to admit, that contributes to development of character among students? Although earlier we found that students attending Templeton-honored schools showed additional growth on dimensions of character compared to students at other schools, when we examined the independent effect of attending a Templeton school the only outcome that was affected directly was volunteerism. The remainder of the effects were mediated through institutional religious affiliation. A large proportion of Templeton institutions (three-fourths) were colleges that are religiously affiliated. As indicated earlier, such colleges can be described as having an institutional culture that provides educational opportunities (curricular and co-curricular) promoting development of values and ethical practices.

Thus much of the positive association observed between attending a Templeton-honored school and character development in college is attributable to institutional characteristics. A higher level of civic and social values development among students attending Templeton-honored schools, for example, is due to students at those institutions tending to be engaged in volunteer work while in college, and it is this specific activity that appears to enhance civic values development. In the same way, part of the positive effect of Templeton-honored schools on volunteerism is explained by students at institutions honored by Templeton entering college with a history of performing volunteer work. Finally, the effect that Templeton schools appear to have on enhancing a student's religious beliefs and convictions is again attributable to characteristics of the student body at a Templeton school. Templeton-honored schools tend to be characterized by a student peer group that is highly engaged in religious activities, and this peer environment contributes to an increase in students' religious beliefs and convictions.

In part, this study was interested in examining the role that schools honored by Templeton play in character development because the schools honored by the Templeton Foundation claim to employ curricular and co-curricular programs specifically designed to contribute to character development. Our analyses, however, allowed us to show that it is not only these institutions that have or potentially can have an impact on character development. All institutions, by offering specific curricular and co-curricular opportunities for students, can contribute to the development of values and behaviors that represent character development in their students. Intentional programming to encourage co-curricular involvement, such as volunteer work, participation in religious activities, interracial experiences, and leadership education, is particularly important in this regard. Campuses can also enhance character development through curricular offerings such as women's studies, ethnic studies, and interdisciplinary courses, which give students the opportunity to discover new truths, become analytical, and integrate disparate aspects of knowledge. Such courses aid in self-awareness, appreciation of cultural complexity, and development of awareness of the many needs of society. Not all of these activities, though present in higher education, permeate or dominate the culture of most colleges and universities. Character enhancing colleges, then, appear to be those that take seriously the many opportunities college has to build character in today's youth.

Appendix: Composite Measures Used in Analysis

Civic and Social Values (alpha = .786)
  Participate in community action program
  Help to promote racial understanding
  Influence social values
  Develop a meaningful philosophy of life
  Be involved in environmental cleanup
  Help others who are in difficulty
Cultural Awareness (alpha = .699)
  Acceptance of people of different races and cultures
  Knowledge of people of different races and cultures
  Ability to work cooperatively
  Understanding of community problems
Volunteerism (alpha = .677)
  Perform volunteer work in college
  Hours per week doing volunteer work
  Plan to do volunteer work after college
Service Orientation of Institution (alpha = .954)
  Many courses involve community service
  Priority to facilitate student involvement in community service
  Campus provides opportunities for community service
  Priority to help students learn how to bring about change in society
  Most students are strongly committed to community service
  Help students examine and understand their personal values
Diversity Orientation (alpha = .893)
  Create a diverse multicultural campus environment
  Hire more minority faculty and administrators
  Recruit more minority students
  Many courses include minority group perspectives
  Hire more women faculty and administrators
  Many courses include feminist perspectives
These composites were developed using a factor analytic technique.

References

Antonio, A. L. "The Impact of Friendship Groups in a Multicultural University." Unpublished doctoral dissertation, University of California, Los Angeles, 1998.

Astin, A. W. *What Matters in College? Four Critical Years Revisited.* San Francisco: Jossey-Bass, 1993.

Bowen, H. R. *Investment in Learning: The Individual and Social Value of American Higher Education.* San Francisco: Jossey-Bass, 1977.

Boyer, E. L. "Creating the New American College." *Chronicle of Higher Education,* Mar. 9, 1994, p. A48.

Chang, M. J. "Racial Diversity in Higher Education: Does a Racially Mixed Student Population Affect Educational Outcomes?" Unpublished doctoral dissertation, University of California, Los Angeles, 1996.

Cress, C. M., Astin, H. S., Burkhardt, J. C., and Zimmerman-Oster, K. "Developmental Outcomes of College Students' Involvement in Leadership Activities." *Journal of College Student Development,* 2001, 42(1), 15–26.

John Templeton Foundation. *Honor Roll for Character Building Colleges: 1997–98.* Radnor, Pa.: John Templeton Foundation, 1997.

Kuh, G. D., and Vesper, N. "The Impress of Different Types of Colleges and Universities on Character Development." Paper presented at the annual meeting of the American Educational Research Association, San Diego, Apr. 13–17, 1998.

Lasker, H. M., and Moore, J. F. "Current Studies of Adult Development: Implications for Education." In *Adult Development Approaches to Learning.* Washington, D.C.: National Institute of Education, 1980.

Levine, A. "Service on Campus" (editorial). *Change,* 1994, 26(4), 4–5.

Pascarella, E. T., Ethington, C. A., and Smart, J. C. "The Influence of College on Humanitarian/Civic Involvement Values." *Journal of Higher Education,* 1988, 59(4), 412–437.

Pascarella, E. T, and Terenzini, P. T. *How College Affects Students: Findings and Insights from Twenty Years of Research.* San Francisco: Jossey-Bass, 1991.

HELEN S. ASTIN is professor of higher education organizational change at the University of California Los Angeles.

ANTHONY LISING ANTONIO is assistant professor of education and assistant director of the Stanford Institute for Higher Education Research at Stanford University.

6

*This chapter explores civic commitment among college
students and offers strategies for how colleges can best
prepare students for a life as a caring and involved
citizen.*

Citizenship Development and the American College Student

Linda J. Sax

The development of citizenship among college students is a long-standing
goal of higher education in the United States (Boyer and Hechinger, 1981;
Colby, Ehrlich, Beaumont, and Stephens, 2003; Finkelstein, 1988; Ketcham,
1992; Morse, 1989; Newell and Davis, 1988). More than two hundred years
ago, education for citizenship was seen as essential to the development of a
well-informed and critically thinking society (Morse, 1989). Although civic
education was somewhat deemphasized during the industrialization and educational specialization of the nineteenth century, citizenship reappeared
as a priority of higher education through the general education movement
of the early twentieth century. Indeed, for many years general education was
seen as a means of safeguarding civic education from curriculum over-
specialization.

By the mid-1980s, however, many educators sensed that higher education was not effectively meeting the challenge of nurturing students' sense
of civic responsibility. As noted in a Carnegie Foundation report, "If there
is a crisis in education in the United States today, it is less that test scores
have declined than it is that we have failed to provide the education for citizenship that is still the most important responsibility of the nation's schools
and colleges" (Newman, 1985, p. 31).

Portions of this chapter appear in Sax, L. J., "Citizenship Development and the American
College Student." In T. Ehrlich (ed.), *Civic Responsibility and Higher Education,* ©2000
by the American Council on Education and Oryx Press. Reproduced with permission of
Greenwood Publishing Group, Inc., Westport, Connecticut.

Since that time, and in particular over the last decade, many colleges and universities have devoted considerable energy to reevaluating their civic functions (Colby, Ehrlich, Beaumont, and Stephens, 2003; Ehrlich, 2000). As evidence, we have witnessed a widespread increase in the number of colleges and universities offering courses focused on "service learning," "problem-based learning," and "community-based learning"—curricular strategies designed to promote students' understanding of and commitment to local, national, and global communities (Colby, Ehrlich, Beaumont, and Stephens, 2003). In addition, membership in the Campus Compact—a coalition of colleges and universities committed to promoting student citizenship through participation in service—has grown to more than nine hundred institutions since its inception in 1985.

This chapter reports on what national surveys of college students reveal about their civic values and behaviors. How does the commitment to civic life among today's college students differ from that of students in the past? How does students' sense of civic responsibility change during the college years? How can colleges best prepare students for a life as a caring and involved citizen?

These questions are examined through the use of data on college students collected by the Cooperative Institutional Research Program (CIRP) at the Higher Education Research Institute (HERI), University of California, Los Angeles. Established at the American Council on Education in 1966, the CIRP is the nation's largest and oldest empirical study of American higher education, involving data on more than eleven million college students at more than eighteen hundred colleges and universities.

Student trends are examined primarily through responses to the Freshman Survey, the CIRP's annual nationwide survey of incoming college students. The Freshman Survey, completed each year by more than three hundred thousand first-year students at some six hundred colleges and universities nationwide, collects data on the background characteristics, attitudes, values, educational achievements, and future goals of students entering colleges and universities in the United States.

Changes in students' civic values and behaviors are examined through longitudinal data collected on college students at three time points over a nine-year period. Specifically, the sample includes 12,376 students from 209 four-year colleges and universities who completed the CIRP Freshman Survey in 1985 and were followed up four and nine years after college entry (in 1989 and 1994). The 1989 follow-up survey includes information on students' college experiences, their perceptions of college, as well as posttests of many of the items that appeared on the 1985 freshman survey. The 1994 follow-up survey furnishes information on graduate school and early career experiences, involvement in community service and volunteerism, and posttest data on many of the attitudinal and behavioral items appearing on the 1985 and 1989 surveys. It is important to note that these data reflect the experiences of students who attended college in the 1980s, before higher education refocused its attention on preparing students for civic life. HERI is currently engaged in new postcollege follow-up of students who attended college in the 1990s. When available, these new data will enable us to assess the extent to which the role of college in promoting civic engagement has changed as this movement has gained momentum in higher education.

Freshman Trends

This section addresses how college students today compare with students in the past with respect to two aspects of civic responsibility: (1) involvement in volunteerism and community service, and (2) interest in politics.

Volunteerism and Community Service. Data from the Freshman Survey show that volunteerism has been on the rise over the past decade, with a record high 82.6 percent of college freshmen in 2002 performing volunteer work during their last year in high school (see Figure 6.1). For many students, volunteering represents more than just a token day at a soup kitchen or a brief visit to a children's hospital. In fact, a full 70.2 percent students who volunteer do so weekly (Sax and others, 2002).

Several factors have contributed to the rise in volunteerism reported by incoming college students. First is the increasing number of service programs supported by federal and state governments (Kahne and Westheimer, 1996; Keith, 1994; Levine, 1994; O'Brien, 1993). Legislation such as the National and Community Service Act of 1990 and President Clinton's National Service Trust Act 1993, as well as numerous city and statewide initiatives around the

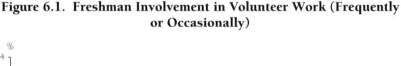

Figure 6.1. Freshman Involvement in Volunteer Work (Frequently or Occasionally)

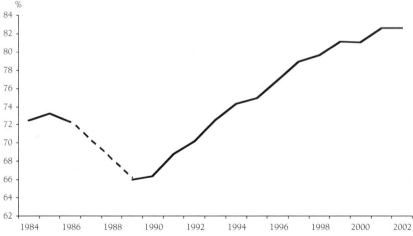

country, have helped to connect more students with service opportunities in the community (Fiske, 2002).

Second is the increasing number of service learning opportunities available at the elementary and secondary levels (Eberly, 1993; Fiske, 2002). An outgrowth of experiential education, service learning is a pedagogical tool that uses community or public service to enhance the meaning of traditional course content. Its connection with specific courses is what distinguishes service learning from other forms of volunteer work. Research has in fact documented that, at least among college students, course-based service has a stronger effect on promoting students' sense of civic responsibility than does service conducted independently or through the co-curriculum (Astin and Sax, 1998; Vogelgesang and Astin, 2000).

A third factor promoting student involvement in community service is the growing number of high schools requiring community service for graduation (Eberly, 1993; Fiske, 2002; Keith, 1994). Indeed, many skeptics assume that the rise in student volunteerism is due primarily to such requirements. However, the fact is that only one in four students who volunteered during their last year in high school attended a school that required community service for graduation (Sax and others, 2002). It appears therefore that the majority of students who engage in volunteer work do so of their own volition.

Interest in Politics. Despite young people's growing interest in volunteerism and community service, their interest in politics has shown a dramatic decline over the past thirty-seven years. For example, the percentage of incoming college students who feel that it is important for them to keep up to date with political affairs dropped from 57.8 percent in 1966 to 32.9 percent in 2002 (see Figure 6.2). Similarly, only 19.4 percent of freshmen say they frequently discuss politics, compared with 29.9 percent back in 1968. Although the overall picture is of declining political interest, it should be noted that following record low political interest among the 2000 entering freshmen, students' interest in politics has increased in each of the last two years. These trends raise two important questions. First, why did students' interest in politics plummet throughout the 1990s? Second, what accounts for the recent reversal of these long-term trends?

Addressing the first question, we learned a great deal from students through student interviews and focus groups conducted during the 1990s. Students reported having negative perceptions of politics and politicians, as well as a sense of skepticism that was no doubt fueled by extensive media coverage of political scandals, negative campaigns, and government gridlock. Similarly, a Kettering Foundation study of college students found that "most everything they have learned about politics, most everything they see and hear involving politics, makes them believe that it is not about solving problems; instead, it is individualistic, divisive, negative, and often counterproductive" (Harwood Group, 1993, p. 5).

Figure 6.2. Freshman Interest in Keeping Up to Date with Political Affairs

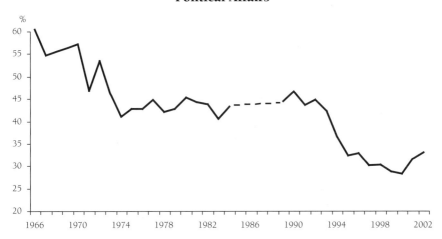

Second, this generation of college students, compared to students in the 1960s and 1970s, is less likely to view politics as an effective vehicle for change (Mathews, 1993; Rimmerman, 1997). As a result, many see no particular benefit in getting involved in the larger political system. Instead, as revealed in the volunteerism trends I have just described, students are trying to make a difference by taking action in their local community.

Finally, college students have reported a sense of disconnection or alienation from the political issues themselves (Reeher and Cammarano, 1997). Unlike students who attended college in the 1960s and 1970s, whose interest in politics was stimulated by issues such as the free speech movement, the civil rights movement, and the Vietnam War, college students in the 1990s generally did not feel that political current events were relevant to their daily lives.

Now to the question of why we have witnessed a small but noteworthy resurgence of political interest in the past two years. Although it is natural to assume that this reversal is due entirely to the events of September 11, 2001, and their aftermath, the survey in fact revealed an increase in political interest over the year prior to September 11. We suspect that this pre-9/11 spike in political engagement was due to the hotly contested and intensely covered 2000 presidential election. It will take a few more years of data before we can firmly establish whether the long-term trend toward political apathy has actually abated.

Analysis of students' left-right political orientation provides additional perspective on the political engagement data. Since the question of political orientation was first introduced on the Freshman Survey in 1970, the number of students identifying as "middle of the road" has risen from 45.4 percent to 50.8 percent. During the same time period, there has been a net

Figure 6.3. Percentage of Freshmen Who Frequently Discuss Politics, by Political Orientation

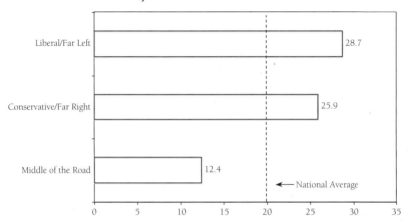

decline in identification with "liberal" or "far left" political labels (from 36.6 percent in 1970 to 27.8 percent in 2002). "Conservative" or "far right" orientations have shown only a modest change over the last three decades, rising from 18.1 percent in 1970 to 21.3 percent in 2002.

Although an increasingly moderate political orientation does not by itself imply "disengagement" from the political process, the data do in fact show that students who consider themselves middle-of-the-road are significantly less likely to talk about politics than those who identify with either a liberal or a conservative orientation (see Figure 6.3). What this suggests is that the politically moderate student is also the more politically disengaged student.

The likelihood of discussing politics also varies by several other student characteristics, most notably students' socioeconomic status and intended college major. For example, 25.2 percent of students whose mother or father holds a graduate degree discuss politics frequently, compared to 13.7 percent among students whose parents never graduated from high school. Similarly, students from families in the top 20 percent of family incomes are one and a half times as likely to discuss politics frequently as students from families falling in the lowest 20 percent of family income (see Figure 6.4).

The most dramatic disparities in political interest relate to students' major (see Figure 6.5). Not surprisingly, students majoring in political science or history show the highest frequency of discussing politics (57.6 percent)—three times more likely than the average college student. Students majoring in English or the humanities also discuss politics at a significantly higher-than-average rate (33.6 and 28.9 percent, respectively). The lowest

Figure 6.4. Percentage of Preshmen Who Frequently Discuss Politics, by Level of Parental Income

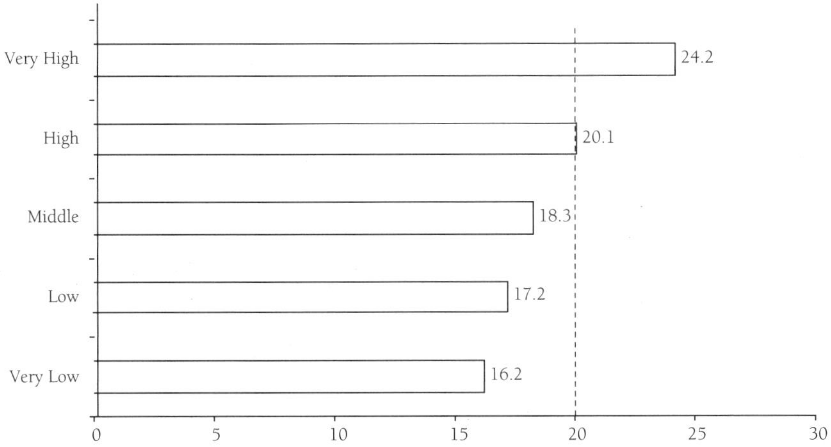

```
Very High  |============================================| 24.2
High       |====================================| 20.1
Middle     |================================| 18.3
Low        |==============================| 17.2
Very Low   |============================| 16.2
           0      5      10     15     20     25     30
```

rate of political discussion occurs among those freshmen majoring in the health professions and education (11.5 and 11.9 percent, respectively). This latter statistic is particularly disturbing, suggesting that it may be difficult to fully reignite students' interest in politics when America's future teachers are some of the most politically disengaged students of all.

Figure 6.5. Percentage of Freshmen Who Frequently Discuss Politics, by Major

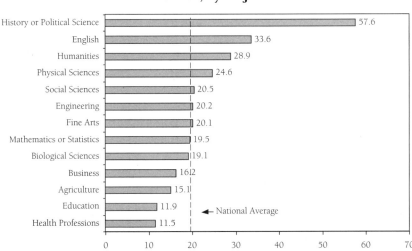

Impact of College on Civic Values and Behaviors

We now turn to the question of the role college plays in preparing students for a life of civic engagement. How do the college years influence students' civic values and behaviors, particularly their interest in and commitment to their community and the larger society? These issues are addressed through an examination of three research questions:

1. How do students' civic values and behaviors change during and after the college years?
2. How are students' civic values and behaviors affected by characteristics of the college environment (institutional size, type, and control; faculty and peer group attributes)?
3. How are civic values and behaviors affected by students' involvement in college (for example, courses taken and time spent on various curricular and extracurricular activities)?

In addressing these questions, the study focuses on three outcome measures, chosen to reflect both the attitudinal and behavioral aspects of citizenship: commitment to social activism, sense of empowerment, and community involvement.

Commitment to social activism is defined in terms of the personal importance the student assigns to certain life goals: participating in community action programs, helping others who are in difficulty, influencing social values, and influencing the political structure. *Sense of empowerment* is derived from students' level of disagreement with the statement, "Realistically, an individual can do little to bring about changes in our society." Students who disagree with this item (in other words, who are more "empowered") can be seen as exhibiting greater potential for involvement in civic life. Finally, *community involvement* is a behavioral measure reflecting the number of hours per week respondents report engaging in "volunteer work/community service" during the past year.

Change During and After College

This section addresses the first research question by describing how students' civic values and behaviors change during and after the college years. Changes in the four components of social activism are shown in Table 6.1. At the point of college entry (1985), 57.3 percent of students considered helping others in difficulty a "very important" or "essential" life goal. During the college years, students' commitment to this goal grew markedly, to 68.1 percent. However, nine years after entering college, this level of commitment dropped to 60.8 percent, representing a net gain in the commitment to helping others of only 3.5 percent over nine years. Similar changes occur for two other social activist goals: to influence the political

Table 6.1. Commitment to Social Activism: Change over Time

	1985	1989	1994	*Change* 85–89	89–94	85–94
Help others who are in difficulty	57.3	68.1	60.8	+10.8	−7.3	+3.5
Influence social values	27.6	45.9	44.6	+18.3	−1.3	+17.0
Participate in a community action program	20.4	29.5	21.3	+9.1	−8.2	+0.9
Influence the political structure	13.0	18.0	13.1	+5.0	−4.9	+0.1

structure and to participate in a community action program. Students show a substantial increase in both of these goals over the four years after entering college, and in both cases the gain almost entirely disappears in the years after college.

Results thus far suggest that the increase in commitment to social activism during the college years may in fact be only temporary. However, there is one measure of social activism for which gains made during the college years are retained in the years after: the commitment to influencing social values. In this case, the dramatic increase in students' commitment to this goal seen during the college years (an increase from 27.6 percent to 45.9 percent) is followed by a postcollege decline of only 1.3 percent.

The second outcome measure, sense of empowerment, exhibits little change during the nine years after college entry. As freshmen, 63.2 percent of students believe "somewhat" or "strongly" that an individual has the ability to change society. This figure increases only slightly—to 66.0 percent—after four years of college. Little change is seen five years later, with 67.5 percent of students reflecting a sense of empowerment. Therefore, unlike commitment to social activism, which grows significantly during college, students' confidence in their ability to make actual changes in society appears largely consistent during college and the years after.

Turning now to our behavioral measure of citizenship, community involvement, we see that Table 6.2 shows the rate of volunteerism among students at three time points over the nine-year period. Involvement in volunteer service is greatest during high school (1985), with 72.1 percent of freshmen reporting participation in volunteer work during their senior year. Participation declines markedly to 35.7 percent during college (1989) and increases to 46.1 percent in the years after college (1994).

The fluctuation in rate of volunteerism led to the question of how much the pool of volunteers actually changes over time. Table 6.3 illustrates the issue of consistency by showing the relationship between prior volunteer experience and volunteerism conducted during and after college. Clearly, having been a volunteer in the past increases one's likelihood of volunteering again in the future. Frequent volunteering during high school more than doubles the likelihood of a student being a frequent volunteer (more than three hours per week) both during and after college. Similarly,

Table 6.2. Rates of Volunteer Participation: High School, College, and Post-College

Level of participation	Percentage of Students
High School (1984–85)	
Frequent	17.4
Occasional	54.7
Not at all	27.9
College (1988–89)	
3 or more hours per week	11.4
1–2 hours per week	14.0
Less than 1 hour per week	10.3
Never	64.3
Post-College (1994)	
3 or more hours per week	15.0
1–2 hours per week	10.7
Less than 1 hour per week	20.4
Never	53.9

those who volunteered three or more hours per week in college were more than twice as likely as noncollege volunteers to frequently engage in volunteer work after college.

Although Table 6.3 suggests some degree of consistency in the volunteer force over time, it also demonstrates a high degree of *in*consistency in who volunteers, since many students who volunteer at one time choose not to volunteer later. For example, among frequent volunteers in high school more than half (54.7 percent) report having done no volunteer work in college, and 46.5 percent report doing no volunteer work after college.

Table 6.3. Consistency in Volunteerism over Time (1985 freshmen followed up in 1989 and 1994)

Level of participation	Level of 1989 college participation (in hours)				Level of 1994 post-college participation (in hours)			
	3+	*1–2*	*<1*	*None*	*3+*	*1–2*	*<1*	*None*
High School (1985)								
Frequent	21.4	13.5	10.5	54.7	26.1	13.1	14.2	46.5
Occasional	9.8	17.3	12.2	60.7	13.5	11.5	27.3	47.8
Not at all	8.9	8.7	6.2	76.3	10.8	8.0	11.8	69.3
College (1989)								
3 or more hours per week	—	—	—	—	21.9	16.5	17.7	43.9
1–2 hours per week	—	—	—	—	26.7	17.2	33.6	22.5
Less than 1 hour per week	—	—	—	—	8.4	14.8	34.1	42.6
Never	—	—	—	—	12.3	7.3	15.9	64.4

Similarly, 43.9 percent of those who reported spending three or more hours per week volunteering in college report spending no time volunteering after college. This marked disappearance of the volunteer force suggests that the habits of volunteerism fostered in high school and in college are quite unstable over time.

The Impact of College

The preceding section establishes that students' civic values and behaviors change during and after college, but it does not explain why such changes occur. This section addresses the second and third research questions by summarizing how college influences each of our three dimensions of citizenship—commitment to social activism, sense of empowerment, and community involvement—in the years after college (as measured by the 1994 follow-up survey). In particular, how are these outcomes affected by characteristics of institutions, curricula, faculty, and peer groups? What role is played by place of residence, choice of major, and various forms of involvement? To examine these college effects, it was important to exert as much control as possible over self-selection (that is, over potentially biasing entering-student characteristics). Preliminary analyses showed that key predisposing factors included a precollege commitment to social activism, prior volunteer experience, and being female. Regression analyses controlled for these early predictors before examining the net effects of college on the three dimensions of citizenship.

Commitment to Social Activism. How does college influence students' commitment to social activism in the years after college? Among characteristics of the college environment, two appear to be particularly influential. First is the positive effect of a commitment to social activism among the student body at an institution (as determined by calculating mean scores on social activism for all respondents at the institution). In other words, regardless of students' precollege commitment to social activist goals such as helping others in difficulty and influencing the political structure, they tend to become even more committed to these goals if they attend a college where other students espouse a social activist mentality.

The second environmental influence on students' commitment to social activism is the negative effect of majoring in engineering. Students who major in engineering are less likely to develop a personal commitment to social activism. This effect is consistent with Astin's finding (1993b) that majoring in engineering is associated with an increase in materialism and conservatism and a decline in concern for the larger society. Findings in the present study suggest that these deleterious effects of engineering persist in the years after college.

Additional effects on the commitment to social activism are the positive effects of time spent attending religious services, performing volunteer work, attending classes and labs, and exercising or playing sports. Students who spend more time watching television, on the other hand, are less likely to develop a commitment to social activism. This latter finding is consistent with earlier research showing that watching television is associated with development of materialistic values and a decline in concern for the well-being of others (Astin, 1993b).

Sense of Empowerment. The second citizenship outcome, sense of empowerment, is significantly influenced by only one characteristic of the college environment: the positive effect of the socioeconomic level of the student's peer group. In other words, attending a college that enrolls students from wealthier and more highly educated families tends to promote students' postcollege belief that individuals have the ability to change society.

Students' sense of empowerment is also positively influenced by several measures of involvement: socializing with people from different racial and ethnic backgrounds, discussing political and social issues, and attending religious services. Conversely, a decline in empowerment results from feeling depressed while in college as well as from the perception that college administrators do not care about student concerns.

Community Involvement. With respect to the behavioral measure of citizenship, community involvement, only one measure of the college environment has a significant influence: the commitment to social activism among the students' peers. In other words, attending a college where other students are highly committed to social activism tends to encourage students' own involvement in their community in the years after college.

Several measures of student involvement during college appear to promote postcollege volunteerism: attending religious services, attending racial and cultural awareness workshops, socializing with students of different racial or ethnic groups, working full-time, performing volunteer work, and talking with faculty outside class. Together, these measures reflect the critical role of personal interaction, whether with students, faculty, coworkers, or employers. Finally, cigarette smoking during college is associated with a lower rate of volunteerism in the postcollege years.

Summary and Discussion

This chapter has focused on the development of citizenship among college students. Citizenship development was addressed through an examination of trends among successive cohorts of entering freshmen, as well as by assessing how students' sense of civic responsibility changes during and after the college years.

The trend data revealed that whereas students today volunteer in record numbers, their overall engagement in the political process remains low (despite the recent small resurgence of political interest). These trends suggest that students are placing their energy where they feel they can make a difference—by getting involved in issues such as education, crime, the environment, and homelessness in their local community. Given their frustration with political scandals and negative political campaigns, students simply may not perceive politics as an effective vehicle for positive change. It remains to be seen, however, whether recent gains in political interest can be sustained, as students in a post-9/11 society assume greater responsibility for keeping themselves informed about political issues and current events.

Next, longitudinal analyses described in this chapter have shown that college is associated with an increase in many measures of civic responsibility. In particular, during the college years students become more committed to helping others in difficulty, influencing social values, influencing the political structure, and participating in community action programs. Such findings are consistent with earlier research showing college to be associated with a gain in altruism and civic responsibility (Astin, 1977, 1993b; Bowen, 1980; Hyman and Wright, 1979; Jacob, 1957; Pascarella, Smart, and Braxton, 1986; Pascarella and Terenzini, 1991). However, findings presented in this chapter show that many of these gains disappear in the first several years after college, suggesting that the effects of college on students' altruistic or community orientations may in fact only be temporary. Further, although the majority of students are involved in volunteer work or community service before starting college, the likelihood of volunteering is significantly lower during college and in the years immediately after. As noted earlier, these results reflect the experience of students attending college in the 1980s. Follow-up data currently being collected on students attending college in the 1990s will allow reinvestigation of this issue.

Finally, this chapter examined how colleges *promote* students' sense of civic responsibility after college. As described earlier, many aspects of the college experience serve to influence students' commitment to social activism, sense of empowerment, and community involvement. Among those aspects, three stand out as being particularly effectual. First is the amount of time students spend in religious services or meetings, which positively influences all three citizenship outcomes. The role of religious involvement is not surprising, given the emphasis on altruism and philanthropy inherent in most religions.

Second is the effect of performing volunteer work during the college years, which enhances students' commitment to social activism and involvement in the community after college. Clearly, forming a habit of volunteerism is critical to the long-term development of citizenship. Nevertheless, findings also show how the pool of volunteers changes dramatically from high school to college, and again from college to the years after. Together, these findings suggest that to build and maintain a volunteer labor force, efforts to promote volunteerism in college should focus as much on retention as they do on recruitment.

A third common theme influencing citizenship development is socializing with students from different racial or ethnic groups, which influenced both the sense of empowerment as well as students' involvement in their community after college. Further, students' likelihood of community involvement was also enhanced by attending racial or cultural awareness workshops. Although positive effects of "diversity" activities have been reported in four-year longitudinal research (Astin, 1993a, 1993b), this study has demonstrated that interacting with and learning from people different from oneself has an effect that lasts *beyond* the college years.

Lastly, college experiences that tend to discourage citizenship development include smoking cigarettes, watching television, and feeling depressed. As a group, these experiences suggest that engaging in relatively isolated or antisocial behaviors tends to inhibit the development of civic responsibility in college students.

In sum, it appears that the development of civic responsibility during the college years is enhanced by students' degree of *involvement* during college—mainly, interacting with students and faculty through curricular and co-curricular activities. These findings are consistent with previous research describing involvement as a key predictor of altruistic values or behaviors (Astin, 1993b; Pascarella and Terenzini, 1991; Pascarella, Ethington, and Smart, 1988).

It is interesting to consider the dynamics of the relationship between involvement and civic responsibility. On the one hand, citizenship development is enhanced by the *nature* of specific activities, such as attending religious services, socializing across racial and ethnic lines, and discussing political and social issues. On the other hand, students who become involved in such activities are likely forming a *habit* of involvement; it is this habit that carries over into the student's life in the years after college.

Therefore, the message to institutions is to provide a variety of opportunities for student involvement, particularly in ways that expose students to diverse people and issues. The more involved and connected students become during college, the more likely they are to seek out forms of involvement in their community after college. In other words, "civic education" is more than simply teaching students "civics." Instead, education for citizenship can be accomplished more broadly by encouraging students to become active and proactive participants in the learning process, pursuing their own interests and making meaningful connections with students and faculty. In this way, colleges can contribute to the development of good citizenship among individual college students while at the same time investing in the long-term welfare of the larger society.

References

Astin, A. W. *Four Critical Years.* San Francisco: Jossey-Bass, 1977.

Astin, A. W. "Diversity and Multiculturalism on the Campus: How Are Students Affected?" *Change*, Apr. 1993a, pp. 44–49.

Astin, A. W. *What Matters in College? Four Critical Years Revisited.* San Francisco: Jossey-Bass, 1993b.

Astin, A. W., and Sax, L. J. "How Undergraduates Are Affected by Service Participation." *Journal of College Student Development*, May/June 1998, 39, 251–263.

Bowen, H. R. *Investment in Learning: The Individual and Social Value of American Higher Education.* San Francisco: Jossey-Bass, 1980.

Boyer, E. L., and Hechinger, F. M. *Higher Learning in the Nation's Service.* New York: Carnegie Foundation for the Advancement of Teaching, 1981.

Colby, A., Ehrlich, T., Beaumont, E., and Stephens, J. *Educating Citizens: Preparing America's Undergraduates for Lives of Moral and Civic Responsibility.* San Francisco: Jossey-Bass, 2003.

Eberly, D. J. "National Youth Service: A Developing Institution." *NASSP Bulletin,* 1993, 77(50), 50–57.

Ehrlich, T. *Higher Education and Civic Responsibility.* Phoenix, Ariz.: Oryx Press, 2000.

Finkelstein, B. "Rescuing Civic Learning: Some Prescriptions for the 1990s." *Theory into Practice,* Fall 1988, 27, 251–256.

Fiske, E. B. *Learning in Deed: The Power of Service-Learning for American Schools.* Battle Creek, Mich.: W. K. Kellogg Foundation, 2002.

Harwood Group. *College Students Talk Politics.* Dayton, Ohio: Kettering Foundation, 1993.

Hyman, H. H., and Wright, C. R. *Education's Lasting Influence on Values.* Chicago: University of Chicago Press, 1979.

Jacob, P. E. *Changing Values in College.* New York: HarperCollins, 1957.

Kahne, J., and Westheimer, J. "In the Service of What? The Politics of Service Learning." *Phi Delta Kappan,* May 1996, 77, 592–599.

Keith, N. Z. "Introduction. School-Based Community Service: Answers and Some Questions." *Journal of Adolescence,* 1994, 17, 311–320.

Ketcham, R. "A Rationale for Civic Education." *Educational Record,* Spring 1992, 73, 19–22.

Levine, A. "Service on Campus" (editorial). *Change,* 1994, 26(4), 4–5.

Mathews, D. "Why Students Hate Politics." *Chronicle of Higher Education,* July 7, 1993, p. A56.

Morse, S. W. *Renewing Civic Capacity: Preparing College Students for Service and Citizenship.* ASHE-ERIC Higher Education Report no. 8. Washington, D.C.: School of Education and Human Development, George Washington University, 1989.

Newell, W. H., and Davis, A. J. "Education for Citizenship: The Role of Progressive Education and Interdisciplinary Studies." *Innovative Higher Education,* 1988, 13(1), 27–37.

Newman, F. *Higher Education and the American Resurgence.* Princeton, N.J.: Carnegie Foundation for the Advancement of Teaching, 1985.

O'Brien, E. M. "Outside the Classroom: Students as Employees, Volunteers, and Interns." *Research Briefs* [Division of Policy Analysis and Research, U.S. Department of Education], 1993, vol. 4.

Pascarella, E. T., Ethington, C. A., and Smart, J. C. "The Influence of College on Humanitarian/Civic Involvement Values." *Journal of Higher Education,* July/Aug. 1998, 59(4), 412–437.

Pascarella, E. T., Smart, J. C., and Braxton, J. "Postsecondary Educational Attainment and Humanitarian and Civic Values." *Journal of College Student Personnel,* Sept. 1986, 27(5), 418–425.

Pascarella, E. T., and Terenzini, P. T. *How College Affects Students.* San Francisco: Jossey-Bass, 1991.

Reeher, G., and Cammarano, J. *Education for Citizenship: Ideas and Innovations in Political Learning.* Lanham, Md.: Rowman and Littlefield, 1997.

Rimmerman, C. A. "Teaching American Politics Through Service." In G. Reeher and J. Cammarano (eds.), *Education for Citizenship: Ideas and Innovations in Political Learning.* Lanham, Md.: Rowman and Littlefield, 1997.

Sax, L. J., and others. "The American Freshman: National Norms for Fall 2002." Los Angeles: Higher Education Research Institute, UCLA, 2002.

Vogelgesang, L. J., and Astin, A. W. "Comparing the Effects of Community Service and Service Learning." *Michigan Journal of Community Service Learning,* 2000, 7, 25–34.

LINDA J. SAX is associate professor-in-residence at the Graduate School of Education and Information Studies at University of California, Los Angeles, and director of the Cooperative Institutional Research Program.

7

Findings from a universitywide values research project connects students' attitudes and behaviors about institutional mission and values to their perceived impact.

The DePaul Values Project: An Ongoing Assessment of Students' Perceptions of a Private University's Core Mission and Values

Joseph W. Filkins, Joseph R. Ferrari

During the summer and fall of 1998, a self-report instrument was developed, piloted, and (over subsequent terms) validated at DePaul University, with the purpose of assessing the relationship between the university's Vincentian mission and its effect on student values. A research team from the Department of Psychology, headed by Joseph Ferrari, devised the initial inventory of eighty-eight statements, and after several factor analyses and logical reinterpretations the inventory was reduced to forty-seven items and named the DePaul Values Inventory (DeVI). Subsequent analyses winnowed the inventory further to twenty-four items (see Ferrari and Cowman, 2004, for a detailed description of scale construction, reliability, and validity testing). This paper presents the results of a subsequent survey as a case study for assessing the students' perceptions of a private university's mission and values.

Funding for this project was made possible in part through a Hays gift on Vincentian Leadership and a DePaul Executive Office and Academic Affairs Fund awarded to the second author. The authors express much gratitude to Fr. Ed Udovic, Shaun Cowman, John Lane, Richard Meister, and J. Patrick Murphy.

Background

DePaul University is a Catholic university in the Chicago metropolitan area serving more than twenty-four thousand students across seven campuses. The university describes its core mission as *urban, Catholic,* and *Vincentian.* The urban aspect is expressed by delivering quality education to locations in and immediately around the Chicago area. The Catholic aspect of the mission is manifested by direct service to the poor and economically disenfranchised through such programs as actively engaging students in volunteer and community service in impoverished urban areas. Murphy (1991) noted that although it is a Roman Catholic school of higher education like other institutions, DePaul University invokes Vincentianism (referring to the namesake of the school, St. Vincent DePaul) through respect for human dignity, diversity and individual "personalism."

The DePaul Values Inventory (DeVI) examines students' perceptions of DePaul University's institutional mission and values along a 7-point rating scale (1 = not at all true; 7 = very much true). Analyses on the DeVI have resulted in four reliable factors, or subscales:

1. *Institutional values education* (eleven items). Students' understanding of DePaul's mission and institutional values found in the university's mission statement
2. *Emphasis on employing diversity* (three items). Students' feelings about the degree to which the university should place an emphasis on recruiting more minorities and women in the faculty and student bodies
3. *Prosocial institutional atmosphere* (seven items). Students' perceptions of the culture and atmosphere at DePaul and whether they feel a sense of altruism on campus
4. *Lifelong commitment to values* (three items). Students' perceptions of the degree to which the values learned at DePaul will continue to influence their life after leaving the university

The items making up each of the subscales can be found in Ferrari and Cowman (2004).

Since 1992, DePaul University's Office of Institutional Planning and Research (OIPR) has administered an annual survey of DePaul's students. Over the years, as the survey grew in size and complexity, a strategy was implemented to annually pose a core set of items about students' experiences at DePaul while focusing on one issue in detail. The issue of focus for the 2001–02 survey was students' perceptions of DePaul's mission and values and how these values are made manifest both in and outside the classroom.

To understand the impact of DePaul's mission and values, we first gauged the students' degree of exposure to mission-related experiences on campus and their perceived benefit derived from those experiences. However, research on understanding human behavior has shown that a person's attitudes and intentions are directly related to his or her subsequent behaviors (Ajzen, 1982; Ajzen and Fishbein, 1977). In other words, the more a person wants exposure to experiences of this type, the more likely the individual seeks out such opportunities. Therefore, a three-tiered approach to studying the impact of DePaul's mission and values was enacted, looking at students' attitudes about such experiences; their exposure to, and perceived value of, such experiences; and finally the impact these experiences might have had on the students.

Thus a three-part survey on student perceptions of university mission and values was devised and administered as part of the OIPR's annual student survey. Using this three-tiered approach, we aimed to gain a more complete understanding of how DePaul's mission and values are manifested on campus and in the students' lives. The three sections consisted of:

- *The DeVI.* Twenty-four items (since expanded to twenty-seven) composing four factors assessing students' perceptions of the institutional mission
- *Behavioral measures.* Twelve university activities asking students to indicate their frequency of engagement and the perceived value
- *Importance ratings.* Thirteen activities and values rated by students on the importance to their lives

The importance measures were used as indicators of student attitudes toward engaging in activities of this type. Since engagement means more than simply going through the motions, we asked students to indicate both the frequency they engaged in, and the perceived benefit derived from, mission-related experiences on and off campus. Finally, we used the DeVI as a measure of impact.

Method

During spring 2002, the annual student survey, including the special section on university values, was sent to a random sample totaling five thousand undergraduate, graduate, and law students. These students had the option of completing a paper version of the survey or an online survey. Approximately one month later, the online version of the survey was opened to any student who wished to complete it. In total, 853 of the 3,000 sampled undergraduates (28.4 percent) and 760 of the 2,000 sampled graduate and law students (38.0 percent) completed the survey. However, an additional 920 undergraduates and 928 graduate or law students responded to the online survey. Thus our dataset comprised 3,409 records: 1,773 undergraduates, 1,476 graduate students, 133 law students, and 27 students of undeterminable level.

Demographically, the survey participants represent DePaul's student population fairly well, with 56.1 percent of participants being female and

64.8 percent Caucasian (compared to 54.7 percent female and 59.7 percent Caucasian in the DePaul population). The percentage distribution across DePaul's eight colleges and schools for the survey participants mapped fairly closely to the population. The analyses were conducted on all survey participants, regardless of their membership in the original sample.

Results

In a previous study, we presented analyses for each section of the survey independently from the others (Filkins and Ferrari, 2003). However, in the life of the university student, such independence is fiction. Interrelationship should be expected between, for example, the degree of engagement in mission-related activities and self-reported scores on the DeVI. Consequently, our focus here is on an examination of the interrelationships between sections of the survey. In so doing, we attempted to answer three questions:

1. Does a more positive attitude relate to more engagement?
2. Does a more positive attitude relate to greater perceived impact?
3. Does more engagement relate to greater perceived impact?

Does a More Positive Attitude Relate to More Engagement? Importance and Value Added. To assess attitude regarding the importance of mission-related experiences in their lives, students indicated the importance to their future plans of engaging in each of thirteen activities. These items were grouped into three goal types, depending upon the activity under consideration (a listing of activities associated with the individual subscales can be found in Ferrari and Cowman, 2004):

1. *Personal values.* Three items asking about the importance of clarifying one's personal values, openness to new ideas, and sense of purpose
2. *Educational and career goals.* Four items asking students about the importance of developing education or career goals, including acquiring a well-rounded education and being well off financially
3. *Relationships with others and society.* Six items addressing the importance of developing relationships and improving local and global circumstances, including being a community leader and working on an environmental improvement project

Responses were made on 5-point scales, with higher values indicating more importance. Indices were calculated by averaging the items corresponding to each goal type to create a single composite mean for each category.

To assess student engagement, we had students indicate the frequency with which they engaged in each of twelve activities, and how much value they thought that experience added to their overall educational experience. These twelve activities were grouped into three categories (a listing of activities associated with the individual subscales can be found in Ferrari and Cowman, 2004):

1. *On campus, course-related.* Activities in which students engaged as part of their coursework at DePaul, including service learning, practicum or internship, and course discussion and projects
2. *On campus, noncourse-related.* Activities in which students engaged on campus but outside of their coursework, including religious services, discussion with students from diverse backgrounds, and student leadership opportunities
3. *Off campus.* Activities in which students engaged outside of DePaul, including community service (specified as independent of coursework), political activity, and environmental projects

Responses were made on 4-point scales, with higher values indicating more engagement or value-added. Indices for each activity type were calculated by averaging the items corresponding to each category to create single composite scores of the frequency and value-added responses. The value-added index scores presented here include only those students who indicated having experiences with the activity type (in other words, if the student indicated "none" for all the items within the subscale, that student was excluded from the calculation of the "value-added" mean).

To study the interrelationship between attitude and level of engagement, students were grouped into one of three groups (low, middle, or high, each encompassing roughly one-third of the students, by level) in terms of the level of importance of the three life goal types (personal values, educational and career goals, relationships with others and society), and students' level of engagement and perceived value added for each activity type was analyzed across levels of importance. For the sake of brevity in this section, only the data from DePaul's undergraduates are presented and only the comparisons for on-campus, course-related activities are presented graphically. Figure 7.1 shows the dramatic increase in the level of engagement and value added as the importance of achieving personal values or relationships with others and society increases associated with participation in on-campus, course-related activities.

A similar pattern was not seen for educational and career goals. From these data, one can conclude that as the importance of achieving the noncareer-related goals increases, the more likely it is the student will engage in and perceive value from on-campus, course-related activities. Although not pictured, differences in participation rate in on-campus, noncourse-related activities were seen across the levels of importance for developing personal values and relationships with others and society. For the off-campus activities, a direct, significant increase in engagement rate was seen across

Figure 7.1. Importance by Goal Type and Participation in
On-Campus, Course-Related Activities

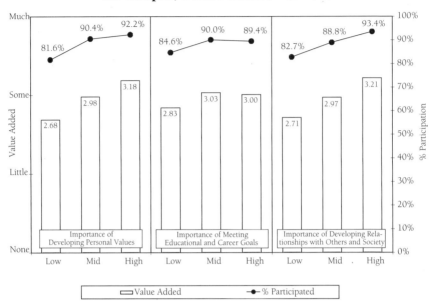

the levels of importance for developing personal values and relationships with others and society.

Does a positive attitude relate to more engagement? It would appear, at least regarding student attitude toward developing personal values and society-based goals, the answer to the question is yes. In addition, student attitudes also seem to affect the amount of perceived value added, suggesting that students get out of the experience what they put in.

Does a Positive Attitude Relate to Greater Perceived Impact? DeVI and Importance Measures. Previous research conducted by the second author (for example, Ferrari and Cowman, 2004) demonstrated that four subscales make up the DeVI: institutional values education, emphasis on employing diversity, prosocial institutional atmosphere, and lifelong commitment to values (descriptions of the four subscales appear earlier in this chapter). Responses used a 7-point rating scale, with higher ratings indicating more agreement with the item. Composite means were calculated across the items within each subscale to create indices, and these indices were used in subsequent analyses.

DeVI subscale scores were calculated across the three importance levels for each goal type, and analyses showed a strong positive relationship between importance and DeVI subscale scores. For example, as shown in Figure 7.2, the more importance the student feels for developing personal values, the higher the four DeVI subscale scores. In particular, the lifelong committed values and prosocial institutional atmosphere subscales show a

Figure 7.2. DeVI Subscale Scores by Importance of Developing Personal Values

DeVI Index Score

| High | Institutional Values Education | Emphasis on Employing Diversity | Pro-Social Institutional Atmosphere | Lifelong Commitment to Values |

Neutral

Low

● Undergraduate   ■ Graduate Student   ▲ Law Student

Little   Some   Much   Little   Some   Much   Little   Some   Much   Little   Some   Much

Importance of Developing Personal Values

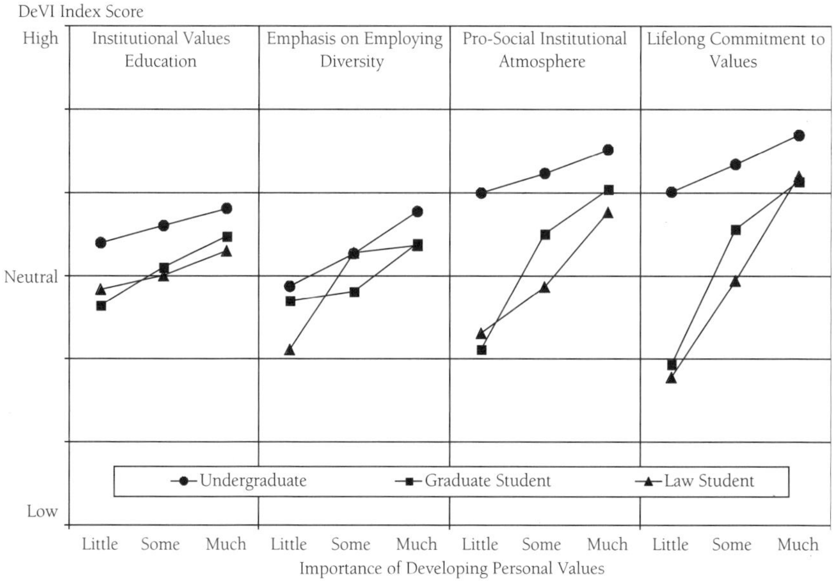

dramatic increase from low to high levels of importance. Typically, undergraduates scored higher than graduate or law students, reflective of the pattern shown earlier. The differences in mean DeVI subscale scores from low to high importance were highly significant (statistically) for all three levels of students, suggesting that more engagement contributes to increases in DeVI subscale scores. Although not pictured, a similar pattern of results was seen for the other two goal types (education and career goals and societal goals), particularly for the altruistic atmosphere and the lifelong committed values subscales. A decrease in the emphasis on employing diversity subscale mean for undergraduates by importance of developing education and career goals was noted, suggesting that career-motivated people are less concerned about this issue.

Does a more positive attitude relate to more perceived impact? In general, these findings suggest evidence of a link between the importance of developing different life goals and scores on the DeVI. In other words, students who have more motivation to achieve certain goals are more likely to have higher ratings on the DeVI. The previous results showed that students who engaged in more mission-specific behaviors also scored higher on the DeVI subscales. The final link would be to examine whether more motivated students are more likely to engage in mission-specific behaviors.

Does More Engagement Relate to Greater Perceived Impact? DeVI and Level of Engagement. To answer this question, students were grouped into one of three groups (low, middle, or high, each encompassing roughly one-third of the students, by level) in terms of their level of engagement with the three activity types on the survey (on-campus, course-related; on-campus, noncourse-related; off-campus). DeVI subscale scores were calculated for students across the three levels of engagement (low, medium, and high).

For on-campus, course-related activities, the analyses showed that students who had more exposure to this activity type typically had significantly higher DeVI subscale scores. For example, undergraduates engaging in these activities also expressed a stronger belief that the university should make more of an effort to recruit women and minorities among the faculty and student bodies. Law students also showed mostly an increase across levels of involvement, but not to the degree shown by the undergraduates. Graduate students, on the other hand, did not seem to have differing subscale scores across the levels of engagement. Similar analyses looking at on-campus, noncourse-related and off-campus activities yielded similar patterns of increase across the four DeVI subscales for undergraduates. However, there were virtually no changes in DeVI subscale scores for graduate students. For law students, DeVI scores fluctuated but showed no consistent pattern. Thus exposure to mission-related activities on campus, whether in or out of class, had an impact on undergraduate perceptions. However, there seems to be limited impact from mission-related activities for postbaccalaureate students.

Figure 7.3. DeVI Subscale Scores by Frequency of On-Campus, Course-Related Activities

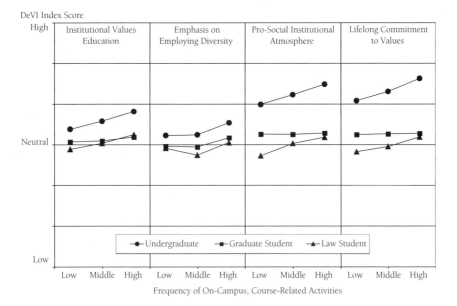

Does increased engagement related to greater perceived impact? These findings suggest that increased exposure to mission-related activities, both in and outside the classroom, is related to heightened perception of aspects of DePaul's mission and values (as measured on the DeVI), particularly for undergraduates. In other words, these findings suggest that with more engagement in mission-related activities, students reported increased understanding of the university's mission and values; increased awareness and acceptance of the institutional atmosphere; stronger belief in the importance of recruiting a more diverse faculty and student body; and increased belief in the lasting impact of DePaul's values on the students' lives after DePaul.

Conclusions

As part of an annual survey of DePaul's undergraduate, graduate, and law student populations, a special section of the survey was devoted to assessing student attitudes toward, their level of engagement in, and perceived impact of mission-related experiences at DePaul. Taken individually, the data showed that undergraduates reported more positive attitudes and a higher level of engagement, and (perhaps) consequently perceive greater impact related to these experiences.

More interesting, though, are the analyses of the interrelationship between the measures from the survey. From these analyses, one could conclude that:

- Students who believed in the importance of working toward mission-related goals are more likely to engage in mission-related activities and perceive the value of such activities
- Students who believed in the importance of working toward mission-related goals had higher scores on the DeVI, a measure of impact of DePaul's mission on students' values
- The more students engaged in mission-related activities, the higher their scores on the DeVI

In short, simply having students engage in mission-related activities may not be enough. Students need to perceive the *value* of such activities, which is in part influenced by (and is perhaps influencing) their motivation to work toward mission-related goals.

Future Directions

The process of exploring student perceptions of institutional mission and values at DePaul University or any organization is ongoing. Students enter and leave the setting, staff and faculty implement varied alternatives, and administrators propose new directions for policies and procedures. Consequently, we continue to explore how students at DePaul perceive the institution (see, for example, Cowman and Ferrari, 2003; Filkins and Ferrari, 2003), including how the DeVI overall is independent of social desirability tendencies and gender differences (Cowman and others, 2002) yet reflective of social engagement behaviors (Campbell, Cowman, Murphy, and Ferrari, 2002). The second author and a team of undergraduate and graduate students explored how DeVI scores related to (1) personal and institutional values, demonstrating that these domains, though related, remain distinct (for example, Cowman, Gors, and Ferrari, 2003); (2) urban and suburban students, who report similar perceptions of the university's values and mission (Gors, Cowman, and Ferrari, 2003); and (3) sense of school community, indicating that among students strong perception of university mission and values relates to strong sense of community.

It should be noted that besides examining student perceptions the second author began a series of systematic studies on staff and faculty perceptions of the urban, Catholic, and Vincentian mission of DePaul University. Although quite exploratory at this point, these projects entail using traditional group surveys and online questionnaires, including a new measure of the institution's mission and values targeted specifically to staff and faculty. Among the factors explored was the relationship for staff between mission and values and sense of school community (Holbert, Collins, Murphy, and Ferrari, 2003). Staff who reported strong affirmation of the university's mission and values claimed strong connection to the school. It should be noted that these relationships were independent of social desirability tendencies or a respondent's claimed faith (Holbert, Collins, Udovic, and Ferrari, 2003). At this time, similar analyses with faculty data are in progress.

Taken together, these research projects (as well as those initiatives currently in progress) at our faith-based institution focusing on students, staff, and faculty reflect the dynamic process of assessment of institutional mission and vales. Our case study is an ongoing assessment process. Moreover, we believe the blending of internal resources (for example, staff from institutional research offices, faculty committed to values education, and interested students) makes similar processes feasible at other colleges and universities—whether public or private. Understanding how all its academic constituents perceive institutional mission and values may lead to development of new policies and procedures as the college and university moves forward.

References

Ajzen, I. "On Behaving in Accordance with One's Attitudes." In M. P. Hanna, E. T. Higgins, and C. P. Herman (eds.), *Consistency in Social Behavior: The Ontario Symposium*, vol. 2. Hillsdale, N.J.: Erlbaum, 1982.

Ajzen, I., and Fishbein, M. "Attitude-Behavior Relations: A Theoretical Analysis and Review of Empirical Research." *Psychological Bulletin*, 1977, *84*, 888–918.

Campbell, A. J., Cowman, S. E., Murphy, J. P., and Ferrari, J. R. "Perceptions of Institutional Values and Mission: Psychosocial Correlates of Social Engagement." Poster presented at the affiliated meeting of the Society for Community Research and

Action at the annual meeting of the Midwestern Psychological Association, Chicago, May 2002.

Cowman, S., and Ferrari, J. R. "The DePaul Values Inventory: Its Utility in Community Psychology." Poster presented at the biennial meeting of the Society for Community Research and Action, Las Vegas, N.M., June 2003.

Cowman, S. E., Gors, T. J., and Ferrari, J. R. "Student Perceptions of Personal and Institutional Values: Similar Structures?" Poster presented at the affiliated meeting of the Society for Community Research and Action at the annual meeting of the Midwestern Psychological Association, Chicago, May 2003.

Cowman, S. E., and others. "Do They Get the Point? Student Perceptions of University Values/Mission Related to Sense of Community." Poster presented at the annual meeting of the Eastern Psychological Association, Boston, Mar. 2002.

Ferrari, J. R., and Cowman, S. E. "Toward a Reliable and Valid Measure of Institutional Mission and Values Perception: The DePaul Values Inventory." *Journal of Beliefs and Values,* 2004, 25(1), 43–54.

Filkins, J. W., and Ferrari, J. R. "Student Perceptions and Understanding of a University's Mission and Values: An Overview of the DePaul Values Project." Paper presented at the annual meeting of the Institute of College Student Values, Tallahassee, Fla., Feb. 2003.

Gors, T. J., Cowman, S. E., and Ferrari, J. R. "City and Suburban Perspectives on Public Service Motivation." Poster presented at the affiliated meeting of the Society for Community Research and Action at the annual meeting of the Midwestern Psychological Association, Chicago, May 2003.

Holbert, C. M., Collins, K. S., Murphy, J. P., and Ferrari, J. R. "Exploring Whether Sense of School Community Impacts on Institutional Values: Staff and Faculty Perceptions." Poster presented at the annual meeting of the Eastern Psychological Association, Baltimore, Md., Mar. 2003.

Holbert, C. M., Collins, K. S., Udovic, E., and Ferrari, J. R. "Spirituality's Place in the Context of Higher Education Employee Perceptions." Poster presented at the affiliated meeting of the Society for Community Research and Action at the annual meeting of the Midwestern Psychological Association, Chicago, May 2003.

Murphy, J. P. *Vision and Values in Catholic Higher Education.* Kansas City, Mo.: Sheed and Ward, 1991.

JOSEPH W. FILKINS is senior research associate in the Office of Institutional Planning and Research at DePaul University, Chicago.

JOSEPH R. FERRARI is professor of psychology at DePaul University.

8

*What is faith development? Can it be assessed? Which
environments and experiences are most conducive to
growth in faith? These are a few of the questions that the
Faithful Change research project attempts to address.*

Faithful Change: Exploring and Assessing Faith Development in Christian Liberal Arts Undergraduates

Gay L. Holcomb, Arthur J. Nonneman

The Faithful Change project was designed to explore and assess the undergraduate faith and spiritual maturation that occurs during a typical student's experience at Council for Christian Colleges and Universities (CCCU) campuses. The CCCU includes more than one hundred members in North America and more than sixty affiliate institutions in twenty-four countries. The CCCU says that "membership in the CCCU requires a strong general education curriculum and majors in the humanities, social sciences, and natural sciences" coupled with a Christ-centered focus (CCCU, 2000, p. 2). The core mission of CCCU schools is to develop the whole person, including not only the intellectual, physical, and social aspects of being human but moral and spiritual dimensions as well. Development of faith, values, and spirituality are the distinguishing hallmarks of CCCU institutions. According to Astin's national studies, published each year since the 1960s by the Higher Education Research Institute at UCLA, students who choose to attend CCCU institutions do so because they want their faith and spirituality to develop. But how do we as CCCU colleges know if we are indeed fulfilling our primary mission objectives? How do we provide evidence to accrediting agencies that legitimately ask us to produce assessment data?

Before something can be assessed, it must first be defined. But definition, much less assessment, of such nebulous and complex constructs as faith and spirituality, is an extraordinarily challenging endeavor. In some respects, it cannot be done. But this should not stop us from doing what we can, making the best use of the tools and instruments that are available.

NEW DIRECTIONS FOR INSTITUTIONAL RESEARCH, no. 122, Summer 2004 © Wiley Periodicals, Inc.

With this in mind, what are some of the characteristics of maturing faith that we in Christian higher education would like to see in our graduates? Keeping in mind that the foundational tenet of CCCU member institutions is integration of faith and reason, basic parameters of maturing undergraduate faith and reason include cognitive, affective, behavioral, and relational components:

- Foundational doctrinal understandings and assent
- An ever-developing relational trust in one's Creator
- Living a life of integrity where one's moral actions flow from one's innermost convictions
- Achievement of one's own personal identity and genuine ownership of one's values and faith
- Cognitive complexity as evidenced by critical thinking skills

Research in faith and spirituality obviously needs to be approached in a spirit of humility, recognizing that we can gain only a partial understanding at best. To do it well, an assessment of faith demands a multipronged strategy that incorporates both measures of content (specific doctrinal beliefs, attitudes, and behaviors) and structural (developmental) components. Neither is adequate in and of itself; both are necessary to get a more complete picture of spiritual development. In addition, both qualitative interview and quantitative survey measures are necessary. Survey questions can answer the "what" questions (that is, what people believe), but only person-to-person interviews can get at the "why" and "how" behind the what.

Designed in consultation with James W. Fowler of Emory University, the Faithful Change project attempts to do just that, incorporating qualitative interviews and quantitative surveys as well as cross-sectional (studying different groups of subjects at one point in time) and longitudinal (studying the same group of subjects repeatedly over a period of time) sampling. The qualitative dimension of the Faithful Change project incorporates the use of Fowler's faith development theory and interview protocol and is the subject of this chapter. The project has been funded in part by a $200,000 grant from the John Marks Templeton Foundation, and a $7,500 discretionary grant from the Lilly Endowment. Additional funding has been provided by participating schools.

Overview of Fowler's Theory

In Fowler's schema, faith, as defined in his most recent book (1996), *Faithful Change: The Personal and Public Challenges of Postmodern Life,* is "meaning making," a generic, universal, and uniquely human capacity. Thus, in Fowlerian fashion everyone has faith—Christian, Buddhist, atheist, and agnostic alike. Faith, in his understanding, is not tied to any particular faith tradition, nor is it content-specific. Rather, it is faith in the universal sense of interpreting the events and relationships that surround us. "Faith, understood in this more inclusive sense, may be characterized as an integral" set of personal principles, "beliefs, values, and meanings that give coherence and direction to persons' lives"; a passionate, yet humble, spending of the self in love; a linkage of "shared trusts and loyalties with others"; "a sense of relatedness to a larger frame of reference" (p. 56); and connectedness to the Holy, the Powerful, the True, the Divine, the Sacred: "People find symbolic representation of this sense of an ultimate environment by seeing their lives as grounded in or related to God. . . . in the love, the awesomeness, and the moral valuing involved in our sense of relatedness to the power and spirit of an ultimate environment, our ways of relating to the world, to our neighbors, and to ourselves. . . . This pattern of our relatedness. . . . to ultimacy we call faith" (p. 21).

Progress into Fowler's more mature levels of faith development requires a fundamental shift in cognitive processing. A transition from one faith stage to another does not necessarily mean a change in the content of one's faith. It does mean, however, changes in how one understands and takes responsibility for living one's faith. In the lower stages, there is a move from the irrational and emotional to the rational, a move from tacit assumptions to explicit ones. If one progresses further into the higher stages, gaining in cognitive complexity, he or she also paradoxically becomes more appreciative of, and open to, the ineffable realms of human experience such as transcendence, love, beauty.

Fowler's work represents a synthesis of philosophical, psychological, and theological insights from Piaget's structural developmental theory (and thus Kant's notion of constructivism); Erikson's psychosocial development theory; Kohlberg's moral reasoning theory; Selman's understandings of role and perspective taking; and the theological contributions of Paul Tillich, H. Richard Niebuhr, and Wilfred Cantwell Smith. To this mix, "he has added structural descriptions of the power and evolution of the bounds of social awareness, the locus of authority, and the form of world coherence—aspects essential to an adequate structural description of the phenomenon of faith" (Parks, 1986, p. 138).

Fowler's Stages

Fowler's theory of faith development includes seven stages (zero through six): "To be 'in' a given stage of faith means to have a characteristic way of finding and giving meaning to everyday life. One has a 'worldview' with a particular 'take' on things. One has a set of values—both conscious and unconscious—that find expression in what one gives priority to in decision making and life planning" (Fowler, 1996, p. 68). Listed in ascending order of development are the seven stages of faith:

1. *Undifferentiated (stage zero)*. During the first year or so of life, initial, vague images of God begin to form in response to caretakers' interactions with the infant. As Erik Erikson postulated, one's ability to trust others is largely shaped during this period of life.

2. *Intuitive-projective (stage one)*. Typical of preschool children, intuitive-projective faith is highly imaginative and impressionable, and largely storied in nature.

3. *Mythic-literal (stage two)*. Although primarily characteristic of children, some adults permanently equilibrate at this stage. Reliance on mystical gut feelings coupled with complete lack of critical thinking skills characterizes such persons.

4. *Synthetic-conventional (stage three)*. "Conforming relationships" with family and peers, emotionally tacit assumptions, and reliance on external authorities characterize individuals in this stage, many of them adults. "Identity, beliefs, and values are strongly felt, even when they contain contradictory elements. However, they tend to be espoused in tacit rather than explicit formulations. At this stage, one's ideology or worldview is lived and asserted; it is not yet a matter of critical and reflective articulation" (p. 61). "Such persons long for harmonious and conflict-free" relationships, and for "warmth and connectedness from their priest or pastor," as well as a parental authority figure. "The underlying metaphor for the church. . . . is that of an idealized or romanticized extended family" (Fowler, 1987, pp. 87–88).

5. *Individuative-reflective (stage four)*. This stage requires one to take a detached, analytical perspective, critically examining values, norms, and ideologies. Concurrent with this advance in powers of reason and logic, unfortunately, come attending drawbacks: a tendency to reduce, to dichotomize, and to see the world in terms of black and white. People in this stage are drawn to the rigidities of fundamentalism (conservative or liberal) and of authoritarian leaders. Typically not humble, they "take into themselves much of the authority they previously invested in others for determining and sanctioning their goals and values" (Fowler, 1996, p. 62). Parishioners functioning at a stage four, individuative-reflective faith have had to contend with "external authorities" and the "internalized voices of parents." Theirs is a rational, explicit, ideological, and owned faith. "The underlying metaphor for church" is "individualism," rational logic, and certitude (Fowler, 1986, pp. 90–91). People functioning at a stage four level focus more on the explicit doctrinal content and how it relates to their ideological stance. They continually question and verify what is said against their own logic.

6. *Conjunctive (stage five)*. In contrast, a person in the conjunctive faith stage "exhibits a kind of epistemological humility. . . . and a principled openness to the truths of other religious and faith traditions. . . . Social perspective taking. . . . at the Conjunctive stage, extends well beyond the bounds of social class, nation, race, gender, ideological affinity, and religious

tradition" (Fowler, 1996, pp. 65–66). People at this stage realize there are no easy answers to the complexities of life. Indeed, this stage brings with it an appreciation for, and comfort with, paradox and mystery. Rigid categories of black and white meld into varying degrees of gray as one embraces both the joys and the sorrows that life extends. Those few functioning in stage five, conjunctive faith "know in their bone marrow that the mystery we name God can only partially be represented in our best symbols and parables" (Fowler, 1987, p. 92). Conjunctive faith rarely develops prior to midlife. It is an earned faith: "earned by having their noses rubbed in our finitude, through the sacrament of failure, and through the death or loss of loved ones" (p. 93). Faith metaphors include words such as mystery and paradox.

7. *Universalizing (stage six).* The ultimate (and rarest) of all the stages, the "Universalizing stage moves beyond usual forms of defensiveness and exhibits an openness based on groundedness in the being, love, and regard of God. . . . Persons of this stage are as concerned with the transformation of those they oppose as with the bringing about of justice and reform" (Fowler, 1996, p. 67). The elite who compose this group include Jesus, Gandhi, Martin Luther King Jr., Mother Teresa, and so on.

As may be obvious, four of the seven stages are not relevant for traditional-aged (eighteen- to twenty-two-year-old) college students. Faith stage zero (primal-undifferentiated) describes infants and very young children (up to age two). Stage one (intuitive-projective) describes young children aged two through six. Stage five (conjunctive) and stage six (universalizing) faiths are not developed prior to midlife, if at all. Therefore three stages remain that are pertinent to the student populations of interest: two, three, and four.

Sharon Daloz Parks (1986) has proposed that the transition between stages three and four, an arduous and somewhat lengthy process, is actually a stage in and of itself. We call this the "3.5 transition." Our hunch is that she is right on target.

Why Fowler's model? Introduced in his classic 1981 book, *Stages of Faith: The Psychology of Human Development and the Quest for Meaning,* Fowler's theory has generated criticism on numerous fronts. But twenty years later, a more viable theory has yet to be introduced. A comprehensive treatise of the strengths and weaknesses of Fowler's theory as well as our rationale for using it is beyond the scope of this article.

However, despite criticism of Fowler for emphasizing underlying psychological structures at the expense of doctrinal content, we have found within the Faithful Change project, to the contrary, that the questions in Fowler's interview allowed us to probe the content of students' faith in a way we would not otherwise be able to do. The Fowlerian stage model constitutes an interpretative framework from which to organize and understand the complex strands of spiritual development. We believe we now better appreciate the texture, richness, and history of students' faith and better understand them as persons of faith. Without a doubt, the insights gained by listening to their narratives have been well worth the additional time and expense characteristic of qualitative research. While reflecting on their past and present spiritual development, students identified those key experiences (that is, times of crisis, hardship, difficulty, intellectual and emotional challenge, exposure to different cultures, service to others) that led both to an attitude of genuine humility and to corresponding changes in their way of thinking and believing.

In addition, the generic nature of the theory has proved to be a strength rather than a weakness for our research purposes. Although most CCCU students are professing Christians, they come from a multitude of denominational cultures. Fowler's model allows us to broadly examine spiritual development from a variety of faith traditions, experiences, and backgrounds.

Research Questions and Methods

In terms of overall project design, in-depth qualitative interviews coupled with quantitative spirituality surveys over time enable researchers to determine spiritual growth patterns, identify when those patterns are most likely to occur, and examine the environments and experiences most conducive to spiritual development.

A total of 240 subjects randomly selected from six liberal arts campuses have furnished, over the four-year span of the study, 600 faith interviews (see Table 8.1). All schools conducted the semistructured interviews using a modified version of the interview protocol developed by Fowler (see Appendix A in *Stages of Faith*). Interviewers were encouraged to probe responses with follow-up questions. Interviews were videotaped and audiotaped and lasted on average approximately 1.5 hours each. In preparations for the first-year interviews, subjects completed Fowler's Life Tapestry (see Appendix A in DeNicola's *1993 Manual for Faith Development Research*) prior to the interview. The Life Tapestry asks subjects to chart key relationships, life marker events, their images of God, and who their respected authorities were at different times in their life. In the fourth and final year of the study, those students interviewed as freshmen in 1998 were reinterviewed as seniors in 2002 after viewing the videotape of their freshman interview. In addition to the standard interview questions, the seniors discussed their reactions to watching their freshman interview. Interviews are coded blindly by two people, per criteria detailed in the manual.

Paralleling the interview, subjects completed the Faithful Change Questionnaire (FCQ), a compilation of various existing spirituality inventories. In addition to the interview and FCQ, all year four subjects completed the Big Five Inventory (BFI) as a measure of personality style. To assess the validity of self-report survey data, FCQ and BFI inventories were mailed out to three people nominated by the student who knew him or her

Table 8.1. Faithful Change Cross-Sectional and Longitudinal Design

Year	Spring
1 (1998-99)	120 freshmen
	60 seniors (cross-sectional comparison)
2 (1999–00)	Original freshmen re-interviewed
3 (2000–01)	Original freshmen re-interviewed
4 (2001–02)	Original freshmen re-interviewed as seniors
	60 new seniors (cross-sectional comparison)

well (parents, close friends, and other family members). In time, these interview and survey data will generate a rich database of spiritual information. It is fully anticipated that distinct response patterns from the various spirituality instruments will correlate with advanced levels of spiritual maturity gleaned from the interviews.

The cross-sectional sample of sixty seniors in year one was included to permit immediate comparison between the faith responses of freshmen and seniors. The second cross-sectional sample of sixty seniors in year four was included to compare the responses of seniors who had experienced three years of in-depth faith interviews with those seniors who had not. In other words, addition of a fourth-year cross-sectional sample of seniors provides information regarding the possible effects of the faith interview as an intervention in and of itself. Students frequently comment that no one has ever asked them questions like this and that the questions have prompted them to think more deeply about what they believe. With few exceptions, most students indicate that it was a valuable experience. One graduating student commented that her senior year interview functioned as a sort of closure for her years of undergraduate experience. Indeed, after observing the positive impact that experiencing the interview typically has on students, one campus has incorporated similar experiences in its freshman and senior core curricula.

Campuses were selected to participate in Faithful Change on the basis of background in research of the participating faculty as well as geographic and theological diversity; each institution is explicitly Protestant and attracts primarily religiously oriented students. Researchers and subjects include faculty and students from six institutions: Asbury College, Kentucky (Methodist-related); Azusa Pacific University, California (interdenominational); Bluffton College, Ohio (Mennonite); Eastern College, Pennsylvania (American Baptist); Eastern Nazarene College, Massachusetts; and Taylor University, Indiana (interdenominational). Affiliate member institutions include Greenville College (Illinois, Free Methodist) and Korea Nazarene University and interdenominational Handong University (both in South Korea).

The Faithful Change project is unique in several regards. First, in terms of research using Fowler's theory it has the largest number of subjects of any research yet encountered (a sample size of approximately 240 subjects from six schools, for a total of approximately 600 interviews). Owing to the expensive and time-consuming nature of faith development research, previous studies have focused on ten to twenty subjects at most.

Second, for the same reasons, longitudinal research using Fowler's model has been rare. Third, although a sample size of 240 may seem small to quantitatively oriented ears, it is unusually large for a qualitative study.

Fourth, although primarily qualitative in nature, initial analysis involves quantitative coding into numeric stage scores, something not frequently done in qualitative research. Fifth, most Fowler research has been restricted to analyzing the underlying stage structure, not analysis of actual interview content. Our analysis attempts to do both: determine stage scores of incoming freshmen and graduating seniors and examine interview content for those key experiences and qualities that are pertinent to varying degrees of faith development.

Preliminary Findings

Cross-sectional year one interview data indicate that the vast majority of freshmen sampled entered college in either stage two (mythic-literal) or stage three (synthetic-conventional) faith, while an intriguing subset entered already at the 3.5 transition. Of the graduating seniors sampled, approximately half functioned at or above the 3.5 level. What is it about these higher-scoring students, whether freshmen or seniors, who reach this 3.5 transitional stage? What are the drivers of their development?

One of the preliminary qualitative findings of this study is that crisis, as understood in the classical Eriksonian sense, is a key driver. Although the term *crisis* may denote emotional upheaval or psychological emergency, it usually does not. Crisis instead refers to a prolonged period of active engagement with, and exploration of, competing roles and ideologies. Used in this sense, crises include anything that challenges people to examine what they believe and why. For development to occur, other beliefs and viewpoints must be not only recognized but also engaged, with a period of critical analysis ensuing. Regardless of the type of crisis experienced, those who enter into such a sustained period of self-examination do so out of recognition of conflict or inadequacy in their own values and reasoning. In other words, they experience cognitive dissonance.

Did close examination of high-scoring interviews evidence such crisis experiences? The answer to this question is a resounding yes. Three categories of crisis were identified: prolonged exposure to diverse ways of thinking, extensive multicultural exposure, and general emotional crisis. Whereas considerable overlap exists between the first two categories, the first involves exposure to people who think differently, while the second involves those who live differently. Incidents were coded as a crisis if they prompted significant reflective examination or if they represented a turning point for the particular person.

The first category of crisis, being around people who think differently or having their beliefs challenged, was evidenced by an overwhelming majority of high-scoring students. These students described being around people who viewed the world quite differently than they did. Several students described being around others who had overtly challenged their beliefs over an extended period of time. For example, some had engaged close friends or family members who were avowed atheists in ongoing dialogue regarding the existence of God. Other students identified specific college classes that had fundamentally challenged their belief structures, particularly science and theology courses.

The second category of crisis, multicultural exposure, was another clear driver. More than half of the high-scoring students had either gone on short-term missions trips, were children of missionaries and had lived in at least two cultures, or had experienced frequent or significant moves while growing up. In each case, the student was exposed to various cultures and ways of living.

The third category of crisis that emerged was a general catchall category of emotional challenges. For example, one student was hospitalized with an eating disorder, another was unceremoniously dumped by a fiancée close to the wedding date, some experienced the death of a friend or family member, and others coped with serious illness in their family.

A subcategory that surprised us was the number of incidences of family mental health struggles. For example, some students reported parents who struggled with severe depression, a parent hospitalized for a nervous breakdown, stepparents who attempted or committed suicide, alcoholic family members, and siblings diagnosed as bipolar (what used to be referred to as manic-depression).

Although the findings reported represent a cross-sectional sampling of freshmen and seniors from year one, we expect these cross-sectional themes to be verified by the longitudinal data. To reiterate, we also expect to find from the cross-sectional sampling of seniors in year four that the interview experience itself functions as a crisis, stimulating deeper reflection. In a manner reminiscent of psychological therapy, the interview questions challenge students to clarify their definitions, assumptions, and explanations. Students are asked to articulate what may seem to be "fuzzy" concepts. For example, the Fowler interview contains such provocative questions as "How has your image of God changed over the years?" or "How do you explain the existence of evil?"

Applying Fowler's Model to Religious Liberal Arts Settings

How can Fowler's model be applied to a religious liberal arts setting? First, Craig Dykstra evidences the kind of critical thinking needed in religious education. Leveling a well-thought-out critique of Fowler's theory and disagreeing with him on many accounts, Dykstra (1986) concludes by writing that although Fowler's faith theory cannot be the core of an approach to religious education, it can be "a useful 'partner' with religious educators" (p. 255). Faith development theory helps us understand "the ways in which such 'contents' of faith are 'structured' and 'processed' by various people in a faith community" (p. 257). "Religious educators would turn first to their own religious tradition as the primary source for its understanding of maturity. . . . and construct the aims of religious education primarily on those grounds. Then they would ask, with the help of faith development theory, what competences are necessary for people to grow into the kind of maturity articulated in those aims. . . . Finally, they would look critically at the aims. . . . to help them inquire as to whether their aims are adequate, or whether, under the stimulus of faith development theory, their aims might be renewed, reformed, and extended" (p. 258).

A crisis offers an opportunity for profound growth and development (Hall, 1986). But it does not invariably promote spiritual and psychological maturation. What distinguishes those who grow through such an experience from those who do not? In essence, environments that foster the appropriate mix of challenge balanced with communal support are the type of environment most conducive to developing a higher level of cognitive, social, and spiritual functioning. Too much of either challenge or support effectively stunts development.

Therefore one goal of Christian liberal arts institutions should be to discover how to create a suitable campus "greenhouse" climate that provides the appropriate balance of support and challenge to individual students. Our campuses need to be perceived as "safe" places in which to explore one's doubts and questions without being unduly judged an infidel. But they also need to be places that challenge our students. We in Christian higher education are too often guilty of coddling our students. Too much or too little of either support or challenge effectively stunts development, spiritual development included.

Summary

The questions addressed by the Faithful Change project have important implications for postsecondary Christian education. Regardless of how individual CCCU campuses delineate spiritual goals appropriate for their particular graduates, we all agree that one of our goals is spiritual growth. If one of the primary objectives of our schools is to foster faith maturation, we need to assess how well we are doing. If one primary reason students come to a CCCU institution is so that their faith will mature, we owe it to our students to better understand their level of faith and what we as educators can do to help stimulate further growth. Overall, pedagogy can be improved through understanding the developmental levels that our students operate from and the transitions they are most likely to encounter during their college years. That same developmental understanding can also inform and enable more effective ministry for chaplains, spiritual life directors, and residence life personnel.

Intended as an exploratory study of faith and spirituality, the Faithful Change project will probably generate more questions than answers. But one of our hopes is that this study will stimulate further research into the development of faith and spirituality on both secular and religious campuses.

References

CCCU Directory and Resource Guide for Christian Higher Education, 2000–01. Washington, D.C.: Council for Christian Colleges and Universities, 2000.

DeNicola, K. B. *1993 Manual for Faith Development Research.* Atlanta: Emory University, 1993.

Dykstra, C. "What Is Faith?: An Experiment in the Hypothetical Mode." In C. Dykstra and S. Parks (eds.), *Faith Development and Fowler.* Birmingham, Ala.: Religious Education Press, 1986.

Fowler, J. W. *Stages of Faith: The Psychology of Human Development and the Quest for Meaning.* San Francisco: Harper San Francisco, 1981.

Fowler, J. W. "Faith Development and Pastoral Care." In D. S. Browning (ed.), *Theology and Pastoral Care.* Philadelphia: Fortress Press, 1987.

Fowler, J. W. *Faithful Change: The Personal and Public Challenges of Postmodern Life.* Nashville, Tenn.: Abingdon Press, 1996.

Hall, C. M. "Crisis as Opportunity for Spiritual Growth." *Journal of Religion and Health,* 1986, 25(1), 8–17.

Parks, S. *The Critical Years: Young Adults and the Search for Meaning, Faith, and Commitment.* San Francisco: Harper San Francisco, 1986.

GAY L. HOLCOMB is a doctoral candidate at the University of Kentucky and research associate at Asbury College, Wilmore, Ky.

ARTHUR J. NONNEMAN is director of institutional research and assessment and professor of psychology at Asbury College.

This concluding chapter reviews some of the methodological issues that analysts need to consider when evaluating the success of character-development programs.

9

Assessing Outcomes of Character-Building Programs: Problems and Prospects

Terrence R. Russell

The chapters presented here make an admirable attempt to apply the logic of outcomes evaluation to programs intended to develop a particular version of "character." The schools and programs described range from deeply religious institutions whose intention and primary mission are inculcation of a specific and global set of norms and beliefs (and where the entire curriculum of an institution may be deemed to contribute to student character development) to public institutions whose character development programs focus on noncontroversial secular values such as social inclusion, individualistic help for the less fortunate (as opposed to organized social action), moderation in all things, cooperation, and conflict avoidance. As we shall see, a good part of the problem of comparing programs across institutions arises from this lack of agreement on—indeed, sometimes flat contradiction about—what is counted as character.

To consider where we may go after these beginning attempts at evaluation, let me review some issues that make application of our ordinary models of evaluation (those that follow as best as possible an experimental design or its parallel regression model) problematic and lead to methodological problems that need to be dealt with. Although character and values exist at a symbolic level and at the level of behavior, we have made methodological choices that lead us to deal less with behavior and more with attitudes, values, and beliefs—more, that is, of what students say than what they do, and even more to the point, with the exception of the surveys developed by NSSE and HERI, what they say they intend to do rather than what they do. There are some issues we must address to develop an adequate model of the institutional or programmatic impact upon student socialization and to bridge the gap between what is said and what is done. A good evaluation design includes the context of the program and its outcomes; otherwise the evaluator (or the program) risks lack of relevance.

Part of this relevance (or its lack) lies in a particular methodological problem for evaluation of character development programs: bias in recruitment and selection, including self-selection. This is a twofold problem in a free market of student choice: the impact of student experience and background and the impact of student aspirations. Especially in the character development area, programs try to attract, and are attractive to, students who are similar to the ones already there, or who want to be like them. It is here that program design and evaluation design may part company. Evaluation design assumes some random variation in students, but character development programs apparently thrive on nonrandomness.

Variation Due to Program Context

In the next paragraphs, the dimensions of this variation important to character programs are discussed in terms of program "context." I chose this route to discussion because I think the issue is not merely one of statistical control over sources of bias. In higher education character development program evaluation, four kinds of context are required, though difficult to document and rarely developed.

Lack of Social Context. There is little or no discussion (let alone investigation) of the source and social correlates of the particular values being promoted. In the case of religious institutions this is not so problematic, but there still exists variation of source (for example, from specific sectarian theology, or from the more amorphous values of what has been termed "civil religion" in the United States). Are values dependent on particular religions, or more functional for a particular social or economic class, or for a particular political group? Do values vary for students with particular intellectual or occupational interests? Particularly glaring is the omission of considering the contemporary U.S. politicization of the very values and behaviors under discussion here, and the decades of on-campus sniping we've come to call "the cultural wars."

We need to consider the sources of social support for a particular value set, but we must also consider the students to whom the programs and curricula are addressed. Is it a guided strengthening of the faith of the faithful, or an attempt to socialize into middle-class society those whose values may be (or are assumed to be) in conflict with that society?

Over the past hundred years, this attempt to socialize has been aimed at a new middle class (see Thorstein Veblen's 1918 description of the University of Chicago in the 1900s); working-class immigrants (see Seymour Lipset's 1996 description of undergraduate life at City College of New York in the

1930s); returning World War II veterans (see Robert Hutchins's views on the GI Bill students, in Simon, 2003); and above all and usually, young men. Whereas historian Ann Douglas (1977) suggested that this target of the character-building effects of undergraduate education dates to the nineteenth century, earlier accounts of bad behavior on the part of male collegians (at least outside seminaries) suggest otherwise.

The bias reported in the contemporary character development program evaluations discussed in this volume points up the overrepresentation of women in participation in almost all areas. Other reports of student life are quite clear on overrepresentation of men in activities that we can charitably call antithetical to character development from the institution's point of view. That this is both an old problem and one whose nature has changed little over the last hundred years is demonstrated by this paraphrased vignette from the biography of Max Weber (Mitzman, 1970), which nicely points out the enduring conflict between the social values officially promoted at undergraduate schools and the young men they educate: Young Max has gone off to Heidelberg to begin his university studies and returns home at the end of his first year. He presents himself at his mother's door. She takes one look at his fraternity uniform and at his beer-swollen face crisscrossed with fresh dueling scars, slaps him hard, and slams the door in his face.

Lack of Life Course Context. By ignoring the very premise of most of these programs—that changes in student values affect values and behavior over their entire life course—we set ourselves a two-pronged methodological trap common in studies of higher education, usually for reasons of expediency and cost: a focus on traditional-age students and late-adolescent socialization, and a focus on immediate student opinion rather than studies across the life course. Longitudinal studies are needed here, as well as some consideration for the maturational processes undergone by older students, who are not usually the target of character programs. As to young men, Erving Goffman's essay on social deception (1969) discusses the role of (especially Oxbridge) higher education in extending adolescence and the functionality of this extension, as evidenced by the zeal and seriousness displayed in an obscure part of World War II clandestine operations: designing land mines that mimic the droppings of animals from around the world. Presumably the socialization of young men does occur eventually, but to determine the role of undergraduate education in this process, we need to follow lives further.

Lack of Role Context. With this almost exclusive focus on programs for four-year undergraduate institutions, there is an emphasis on the student role as global rather than merely one of a complicated and highly variable set of roles. This is exacerbated by a focus on the institution as the unit of analysis that does not (usually for good research design reasons!) allow disaggregation by major or consider other roles of the individual as sources for values education. There is an overattribution of causality to the college experience in general and character development programs (because of partial participation) in particular. Of special note is the amount of time undergraduates spend working.

Related to the idea of studying the broader role set of students is an older concept of character as a deep, unarticulated, "understood" set of values, norms, and expectations that formed the background of explicit role relationships and mutual obligations. This tradition ties character firmly to the concept of community, neatly expressed by Thomas and Znaniecki's translation of the observation of an early twentieth-century Polish peasant, that a man's community stretches as far as his reputation (1958). Emile Durkheim (1964) referred to the remains of this older version of community in modern society as the "non-contractual basis of the contract"; sociologist Robert Nisbet (1990) referred to the relational "space between" the explicit web of interpersonal connections that made for community, the social expression of character.

This concept of character raises an interesting point for program development and evaluation: How do you create a formal program to teach these values, norms, and expectations? The answer seems to lie in experiential programs, where character emerges indirectly as a part of the growth of community among relatively small groups of students who are spending time together. Several examples come to mind: development of a scientific research group; the residential house system and the experiences at Deep Springs College; and the late, lamented Black Mountain College. The learning community movement has spawned so many structural variations that it is not easily included in this group.

Lack of Historical and Cognitive Context. The proponents of character development programs seek the same ends as those we used to associate with the liberal arts and sciences, which have been marginalized to the point where teaching and learning is seen as purely information transfer within a set of professional (for example, employment-related) curricula. It appears that the need for character development programs is a response to the decline of the liberal arts, sciences, and humanities (LA&S) occasioned by several related changes in undergraduate education. First, the shift of students into employment-related major programs such as engineering, business, education, and nursing (coupled with a rise in the number of hours spent working, as mentioned earlier) reduced the number of opportunities for students to take LA&S courses, as is chronicled by Clifford Adelman in *Tourists in Our Own Land* (1992). Second, the transformation of the humanities into technical social sciences left little residue in the classroom of the more traditional humanities pursuit of the development of critical modes of thought, consideration for rules of inquiry and evidence, and general consideration of the question, "How shall we live?" As the bearer of questions and modes of thinking about them, the humanities have historically been part of the secular, liberating program of LA&S, generally standing in opposition to the programs of sacred answers to the same questions.

Summary

To summarize recommendations for evaluating character development programs:

- Take care when aggregating, especially if you are using the institution as the unit of analysis. The two comparative studies (NSSE and HERI) are useful for giving some direction in sorting out the most important types of role context for character program evaluation, particularly where the institution is the unit of analysis. These studies used national surveys to infer character development or activities that may lead to character development. This strengthens the ability to compare institutions, but it blurs valid differences between various institutional character development goals, by comparing faith development programs in religious institutions with civic values development programs in secular institutions.
- To deal with social context issues, it would be useful, as part of a character development program, to spend some time placing character and program goals in the broader context of a range of social values tied to specific social groups and structures. Be explicit about whose values are being promulgated and who the target audience is.
- To deal with life course context issues, a program should consider investing resources in longitudinal studies of alumni as a method for truly evaluating the impact of character education on life values.
- To deal with role context issues, a program should develop a good sense of how much time students spend in program activities (the NSSE approach is good, or a time budget approach) and a sense of the comparative saliency of other roles (work, family, and so on) in character development.
- To place a character development program within an institutional historical and cognitive context, a review of the content of the academic curriculum would help identify those places where character development is an informal benefit of the process of other learning, and also help identify the content of such character development.
- Keep in mind that these are messy problems indeed, and there will be only satisficing solutions, unless we wish to give up the evaluative enterprise altogether.

Looking to the future, I think that the issues discussed in this volume will loom larger on the undergraduate education scene as both character development programs and assessment become more widespread. Character development programs will increase in number because of the need for late adolescent and early adult middle-class socialization and because the advent of mass undergraduate education coupled with the decline of alternative experiences (the military, work apprenticeship, the *Wanderjahr*) means that colleges are ever more important to this process. The explosion of interest in the NSSE and HERI work in this area is a good indicator of the future. Assessment of undergraduate outcomes is no longer solely the interest of administrators and those who love testing and measurement; it has become a way of life in many institutions, driven by a need to explain the impact of the education process to the business and legislative communities who want in the first instance a metric for employee selection and in the second a metric for input-output calculations of efficiency in that process. Together, these two trends tie undergraduate education more firmly to the larger world—an unexpected outcome for a matching of the "softest" and "hardest" trends in higher education.

References

Adelman, C. *Tourists in Our Own Land: Cultural Literacies and the College Curriculum.* Washington, D.C.: U.S. Department of Education, Oct. 1992.

Douglas, A. *The Feminization of American Culture.* New York: Knopf, 1977.

Durkheim, E. *The Division of Labor in Society* (G. Simpson, trans.). New York: Free Press of Glencoe, 1964.

Goffman, E. *Strategic Interaction.* Philadelphia: University of Pennsylvania Press, 1969.

Lipset, S. "Steady Work: An Academic Memoir." *Annual Review of Sociology,* 1996, 22, 1–27.

Mitzman, A. *The Iron Cage: An Historical Interpretation of Max Weber.* New York: Knopf, 1970.

Nisbet, R. *The Quest for Community: A Study in the Ethics of Order and Freedom.* San Francisco: Institute for Contemporary Studies Press, 1990.

Simon, P. "Point of View: A GI Bill for Today." *Chronicle of Higher Education,* Oct. 31, 2003, p. B16.

Thomas, W., and Znaniecki, F. *The Polish Peasant in Europe and America, Vol. I.* New York: Dover, 1958.

Veblen, T. *The Higher Learning in America: A Memorandum on the Conduct of Universities by Business Men.* New York: Huebsch, 1918.

TERRENCE R. RUSSELL *is executive director of the Association for Institutional Research at the Florida State University.*

INDEX

Back Issue/Subscription Order Form

Copy or detach and send to:

Jossey-Bass, A Wiley Imprint, 989 Market Street, San Francisco CA 94103-1741

Call or fax toll-free: Phone 888-378-2537 6:30AM – 3PM PST; Fax 888-481-2665

Back Issues: Please send me the following issues at $29 each
(Important: please include ISBN number with your order.)

_____

_____

_____

$ _____ Total for single issues

$ _____ SHIPPING CHARGES: SURFACE Domestic Canadian

	Domestic	Canadian
First Item	$5.00	$6.00
Each Add'l Item	$3.00	$1.50

For next-day and second-day delivery rates, call the number listed above.

Subscriptions Please __ start __ renew my subscription to *New Directions for Institutional Research* for the year 2_____ at the following rate:

U.S.	__ Individual $80	__ Institutional $160
Canada	__ Individual $80	__ Institutional $200
All Others	__ Individual $104	__ Institutional $234
Online Subscription		__ Institutional $160

**For more information about online subscriptions visit
www.wileyinterscience.com**

$ _____ Total single issues and subscriptions (Add appropriate sales tax for your state for single issue orders. No sales tax for U.S. subscriptions. Canadian residents, add GST for subscriptions and single issues.)

__Payment enclosed (U.S. check or money order only)

__VISA __ MC __ AmEx # _____ Exp. Date _____

Signature _____ Day Phone _____

__ Bill Me (U.S. institutional orders only. Purchase order required.)

Purchase order # _____
Federal Tax ID13559302   GST 89102 8052

Name _____

Address _____

_____

Phone _____ E-mail _____

For more information about Jossey-Bass, visit our Web site at www.josseybass.com

hierarchical linear modeling to measure pay equity. They present a case-study approach to illustrate the political and practical challenges that researchers often face when conducting a salary-equity study for an institution. This is a companion volume to Conducting Salary-Equity Studies: Alternative Approaches to Research (IR115).
ISBN: 0-7879-6863-3

IR116 **Reporting Higher Education Results: Missing Links in the Performance Chain**
Joseph C. Burke, Henrick P. Minassians
The authors review performance reporting's coverage, content, and customers, they examine in depth the reporting indicators, types, and policy concerns, and they compare them among different states' reports. They highlight weaknesses in our current performance reporting—such as a lack of comparable indicators for assessing the quality of undergraduate education—and make recommendations about how to best use and improve performance information.
ISBN: 0-7879-6336-4

IR115 **Conducting Salary-Equity Studies: Alternative Approaches to Research**
Robert K. Toutkoushian
Synthesizing nearly 30 years of research on salary equity from the field of economics and the experiences of past studies, this issue launches an important dialogue between scholars and institutional researchers on the methodology and application of salary-equity studies in today's higher education institutions. The first of a two-volume set on the subject, it also bridges the gap between academic research and the more pragmatic statistical and political considerations in real-life institutional salary studies.
ISBN: 0-7879-6335-6

IR114 **Evaluating Faculty Performance**
Carol L. Colbeck
This issue brings new insights to faculty work and its assessment in light of reconsideration of faculty work roles, rapid technological change, increasing bureaucratization of the core work of higher education, and public accountability for performance. Exploring successful methods that individuals, institutions, and promotion and tenure committees are using for evaluations of faculty performance for career development, this issue is an indispensable guide to academic administrators and institutional researchers involved in the faculty evaluation process.
ISBN: 0-7879-6334-8

IR113 **Knowledge Management: Building a Competitive Advantage in Higher Education**
Andreea M. Serban, Jing Luan
Provides a comprehensive discussion of knowledge management, covering its theoretical, practical, and technological aspects with an emphasis on their relevance for applications in institutional research. Chapters examine the theoretical basis and impact of data mining; discuss the role of institutional research in customer relationship management; and provide a framework for the integration of institutional research within the larger context of organization learning. With a synopsis of technologies that support knowledge management and an exploration of future developments in this field, this volume assists institutional researchers and analysts in taking advantage of the opportunities of knowledge management and addressing its challenges.
ISBN: 0-7879-6291-0

IR112   **Balancing Qualitative and Quantitative Information for Effective Decision Support**
Richard D. Howard, Kenneth W. Borland Jr.
Establishes methods for integration of numeric data and its contextual application. With theoretical and practical examples, contributors explore the techniques and realities of creating, communicating, and using balanced decision support information. Chapters discuss the critical role of measurement in building institutional quality; examples of conceptual and theoretical frameworks and their application for the creation of evaluation information; and methods of communicating data and information in relation to its decision support function.
ISBN: 0-7879-5796-8

IR111   **Higher Education as Competitive Enterprise: When Markets Matter**
Robert Zemsky, Susan Shaman, Daniel B. Shapiro
Offers a comprehensive history of the development and implementation of Collegiate Results Instrument (CRI), a tool for mapping the connection between market forces and educational outcomes in higher education. Chapters detail the methods that CRI uses to help institutions to remain value centered by becoming market smart.
ISBN: 0-7879-5795-X

IR110   **Measuring What Matters: Competency-Based Learning Models in Higher Education**
Richard Voorhees
An analysis of the findings of the National Postsecondary Education Cooperative project on data and policy implications of national skill standards, this issue provides researchers, faculty, and academic administrators with the tools needed to deal effectively with the emerging competency-based initiatives.
ISBN: 0-7879-1411-8

IR109   **The Student Ratings Debate: Are They Valid? How Can We Best Use Them?**
Michael Theall, Philip C. Abrami, Lisa A. Mets
Presents a thorough analysis of the use of student evaluations of teaching for summative decisions and discusses the ongoing controversies, emerging research, and dissenting opinions on their utility and validity. Summarizes the role of student ratings as tools for instructional improvement, as evidence for promotion and tenure decisions, as the means for student course selection, as a criterion of program effectiveness, and as the continuing focus of active research and intensive discussion.
ISBN: 0-7879-5756-9

IR108   **Collaboration Between Student Affairs and Institutional Researchers to Improve Institutional Effectiveness**
J. Worth Pickering, Gary R. Hanson
Defines the unique aspects of student affairs research, including its role in responding to assessment mandates and accreditation agencies, its use of student development theory in formulating research questions, the value of qualitative methods it employs, and the potential contribution it can make to institutional decision making.
ISBN: 0-7879-5727-5

IR107 **Understanding the College Choice of Disadvantaged Students**
Alberto F. Cabrera, Steven M. La Nasa
Examines the college-choice decision of minority and disadvantaged students and suggests avenues to help promote access and improve participation. Explores the influence of family and high school variables as well as racial and ethnic differences on college-choice.
ISBN: 0-7879-5439-X

IR106 **Analyzing Costs in Higher Education: What Institutional Researchers Need to Know**
Michael F. Middaugh
Presents both the conceptual and practical information that will give researchers solid grounding in selecting the best approach to cost analysis. Offers an overview of cost studies covering basic issues and beyond, from a review of definitions of expenditure categories and rules of financial reporting to a discussion of a recent congressionally mandated study of higher education costs.
ISBN: 0-7879-5437-3

IR105 **What Contributes to Job Satisfaction Among Faculty and Staff**
Linda Serra Hagedorn
Argues that positive outcomes for the entire campus can only be achieved within an environment that considers the satisfaction of all of those employed in the academy. Examines various jobs within the campus community— including classified staff and student affairs administrators as well as faculty— and suggests factors that will promote job satisfaction.
ISBN: 0-7879-5438-1

IR104 **What Is Institutional Research All About? A Critical and Comprehensive Assessment of the Profession**
J. Fredericks Volkwein
Chapters explore the role IR plays in improving an institution's ability to learn, review organizational behavior theories that shed light on the researcher's relationship with the institution, and discuss the three tiers of organizational intelligence that make up IR—technical/analytical, contextual, and issues intelligence.
ISBN: 0-7879-1406-1

IR103 **How Technology Is Changing Institutional Research**
Liz Sanders
Illustrates how to streamline office functions through the use of new technologies, assesses the impact of distance learning on faculty workload and student learning, and responds to the new opportunities and problems posed by expanding information access.
ISBN: 0-7879-5240-0

IR102 **Information Technology in Higher Education: Assessing Its Impact and Planning for the Future**
Richard N. Katz, Julia A. Rudy
Provides campus leaders, institutional researchers, and information technologists much-needed guidance for determining how IT investments should be made, measured, and assessed. Offers practical, effective models for integrating IT planning into institutional planning and goals, assessing the impact of IT investments on teaching, learning, and administrative operations, and promoting efficient information management practices.
ISBN: 0-7879-1409-6